THE PRINTING OF BOOKS

THE PRINTING
OF BOOKS

HOLBROOK JACKSON

Essay Index Reprint Series

BOOKS FOR LIBRARIES PRESS
FREEPORT, NEW YORK

First Published 1939
Reprinted 1970

Z
116
A3J33
1970

INTERNATIONAL STANDARD BOOK NUMBER:
0-8369-1931-9

LIBRARY OF CONGRESS CATALOG CARD NUMBER:
70-134100

PRINTED IN THE UNITED STATES OF AMERICA

CONTENTS

I. PRINTING FOR READING

II. THE AUTHOR AND HIS PRINTER

III. OCCASIONAL PAPERS

LIST OF ILLUSTRATIONS

PART I

PRINTING FOR READING

I

TYPOPHILIA

TYPOPHILIA OR THE LOVE OF PRINTING FOR ITS OWN SAKE must in the end justify itself by the amount of satisfaction it gives to the reader. It will be challenged only when it affects the proper relationship of reader and printer. That relationship has been fixed for all time by the main purpose of a book, which is to be read. If at any time the printer asserts himself at the expense of the reader, becomes puffed up with pride at his own artistry so that his work struts between what the author has written and what the reader would read, he must be put back into his proper place.

Some typophils so revere beauty of design that a book made for reading is gloated upon for its physical charms alone. With such enthusiasts reading is often a secondary attraction, and, in aggravated cases, it may become negligible or even unnecessary. Inadequate as such a taste will seem to authors and readers it is nothing compared with those excessive passions which focus affection upon the parts of a book: title-page, binding, initials, tailpieces, &c., as lovers may augment passion by idealizing some detached feature or possession of the beloved one. There are many who do not hesitate to class enthusiasts of this kind among the demented; yet, without such fierce and excluding affections, it is certain that numbers of the fine books of times past would have been destroyed by the carelessness of scholars or worn out by clumsy readers.

It is usual, however, for typophils to prefer a more balanced amatory diet, and the more normal lovers of print like to relate their affection to the whole of a book rather than confine it to a part. There is a growing number of readers in these times of ample choice who appreciate the design of books, although, as Stanley Morison reminds us, the 'enjoyment of patterns is rarely the reader's chief aim'. Authentic readers seldom become large-scale collectors, but they are not averse from permitting specimens of the more ambitious kind of designed books to associate with their workaday copies. But whether they are readers or collectors, or both, an assembly of comely books justifies itself by expressing the taste of the owner and honouring alike the arts of authorship and printing.

If literature and typography have been enriched by the enthusiasm of collectors it is because those collectors had a passion for books as books rather than any particular taste for style in writing or printing. They prefer ready-made standards as exemplified in famous books, or, when they are interested in typography, it is in 'fine printing'. And since difficulty of acquisition is a stimulus to the possessive sense, they seldom become enamoured of a book unless it is rare, or unless they believe it will become rare.

There is, however, another kind of collector who is perhaps even more important than the Paladin of rarity. It is he who regards typography as part of the ritual of literature, and believes that a book can be a work of art like a picture, a statue, or a garden : that a book is not only for inward but for outward contemplation, and that the excellences of its material parts are a tribute to its qualities as a piece of writing. By his taste and devotion he is not only preserving from destruction some of the loveliest of made things, he is celebrating the genius which inspired them. It is by such homage that books, like altars, became shrines for exuberant decoration.

Printing has something of the inevitability of art. It did not grow up: the craft which that great English printer, John Baskerville, called 'the most useful Art known to mankind' was born adult and, unlike many inventions, it had not to fight for a living. The convenience of printing was instantly recognized and, since the trend of civilization has more often been determined by inventions than by ideas or policies or principles, the widespread acceptance of printing has given books and other printed documents an important place in ethnology. You can read history in type-faces alone, and it may be discovered one of these days that printing types are a key to the understanding of cultural and even racial types. The ideograph, for instance, may have fixed Chinese civilization just as the use of roman types in the fifteenth century released forces which started the Western world upon a new adventure. But it is more certain that with the invention of movable types the varied and mobile civilization we know became inevitable. Francis Bacon observed that printing was one of the inventions which separated the ancient from the modern world; and it is significant that among the other influences he does not include ideas but devices, like gunpowder and the magnet.[1] 'No star', he says, 'seems to have exerted greater power and influence in human affairs than that of mechanical discoveries.' But of all mechanical discoveries printing has been the most influential because its power has been continuous and cumulative. As the preserver of ideas and thoughts, *ars artium omnium conservatrix*,[2] printing is amply recognized. 'Sir', said Dr. Johnson with hyperbolical emphasis, 'if it had not been for the art of printing, we should now have no learning at all; for books would have perished faster than they could have been transcribed.'

Whether printing has always been for the best is sometimes doubted, and with reason, for so accessible a medium of expression is exposed to misuse by self-interested and predatory, as well as by stupid, people. The periodical press has always been suspect, but it has had respectable supporters as well. Samuel Butler said that 'the most important service rendered by the press and the magazine is that of educating people to approach printed matter with distrust'.[3] Samuel Johnson not only believed that 'the mass of every people must be barbarous where there is no printing', but that the English 'vulgar' were superior to the Greek and Roman 'masses' because they 'had the advantage of such knowledge as was diffused by the newspapers'.[4] Each attitude has so much corroborating evidence that most educated people will prefer

1 See Notes, p. 267, *infra*.   2 'The art preservative of all arts.' Motto on the house of Laurent Koster at Haarlem.   3 *Further Extracts from the Note-Books of Samuel Butler* (1934), 261.   4 *Boswell's Life*, ed. Hill (1887), ii. 170. See also *Idler*, 7.

to sit on the fence with William Cowper and see in the press a 'fountain, at which drink the good and wise', as well as an 'ever-bubbling spring of endless lies'.

Print is not only the most convenient method of making intellectual and imaginative contacts, it is also the most permanent. Deep registration depends upon repetition. Communication of ideas is not enough. Language is a slow creator until it is printed. It is not enough to put ideas into words. Words must be recorded and copied and circulated continuously, and subjected to the consideration and reflection and discussion of all manner of folk, wise and unwise, learned and profane, before they can claim common recognition. Yet once ideas are printed they stick like burrs. We quickly forget what we hear by radio; the talkies tell us only what we already know, and oratory often leaves us with a more vivid idea of the orator than of what he said. Speeches and radio talks have to resort to print if they desire permanent repute or widespread effect. It is the press, not the platform, that makes the reputations of politicians, and so with ideas in general, for books never weary of repeating themselves. The patient iteration of print may not always be immediately effective, but like an underground river there is no knowing when what has been printed will gush forth and become part of both the intellectual and the emotional landscapes.

The dangers of printing, as our pastors and masters are aware, are not confined to misrepresentation, and frankness in print can be more troublesome than prevarication. Efforts are always being made to limit the freedom of the press when truth clashes with established opinion, or expression gets too far ahead of convention. No greater compliment could be paid to its potency. But although you may repress the printed word, you cannot suppress it, for once a thought is printed, whether it is a good thought or a bad thought, it lives for ever. In many countries even at the present time raids are made upon books and periodicals on religious, moral, or political grounds, and in most countries you are only permitted to print what you like if your thoughts happen to coincide with the ideas or policies of large interests in religion, morals, politics, or finance. There are vested interests in ideas as well as in things.

What better occupation then for the collector than the assembling of little libraries which illustrate the developments and permutations of this powerful and fearful craft. Not the formation of collections which exhibit the evolution of printing from the fourteen hundreds to the nineteen hundreds. That would be too obvious a task even if one's purse were deep enough. Such assemblies are for State or Municipality, or University, not for the private bookman; and it is doubtful whether they are as interesting or even as valuable as the lesser spurts and digressions, each revealing characteristics and excellences or even eccentricities. Nothing is so tiresome as insistence upon the idea of a continuous evolution, especially of books. How much better to feel that adventurous and imaginative bookmen are creating constellations of their own, as individual in their way as the apparently autonomous star clusters that sparkle in the night.

At one time collectors, who by the way are not always infallible guides to what is excellent, looked to the past for typographical treasures:

> Art stopped short at the cultivated Court
> of the Empress Josephine . . .

or very much earlier. A hundred years ago there was a mania for books printed in Gothic characters. Collectors avidly sacrificed typographical charm (or even fitness) to antiquarian glamour:

> Who dreams, the *Type* should please us all,
> That 's not too thin, and not too tall,
> Nor much awry, nor over small,
> And, if *but* Roman, asks no better—
> May die in darkness:—I, for one,
> Disdain to tell the barb'rous Hun,
> That Persians but adore the Sun,
> Till taught to know *our* God . . . 𝕭𝖑𝖆𝖈𝖐 𝕷𝖊𝖙𝖙𝖊𝖗.[1]

Book collectors have begun to realize that Gutenberg and Caxton, and other fathers of printing, were navigators in an illimitable sea. Between their time and ours there have been typographical adventures innumerable, and the treasures left by the later are not less interesting, or even less precious, than those discovered by earlier explorers. Our own land has produced delectable and collectable printers and typographers, and not alone fastidious or eccentric amateurs like Horace Walpole, Egerton Brydges, and C. H. O. Daniel, William Morris, and St. John Hornby.

The collector of works illustrating the art of printing

---

1 *Bibliosophia* [James Beresford] (1810), vii.

no longer confines his attention either to the curious specimens of the amateur or the splendours of the old masters. In modern times there have been masters also: John Baskerville of Birmingham and the Foulis brothers of Glasgow, whose books express the typographical genius of a century of patricians. They are followed by the great trade printers William Bulmer, Richard Bensley, and Charles Whittingham of London and James Ballantyne of Edinburgh. Good printing is no longer the monopoly of private presses. We have entered a new typographical era and the commercial printer having learnt his lesson from the amateur is now producing books which would be distinguished even among the masterpieces of the past.

Favouritism and exaggeration are familiar vices of collecting. By excessive spot-lighting the powerful amateur and his commercial imitator have often undermined the normal processes of good taste. Taste also is the victim of booms and slumps. There are fashions in print as in other merchandise, and the novice often fails to realize that these fashions are no more than commercial tricks. Yet even fashions are interesting to the investigator, and collectors serve a useful purpose by preserving and recording examples of modish typography which will be appreciated by historians and sociologists.

It is the privilege of the observant book-collector who is a connoisseur and not merely a hoarder to sort out tendencies and to show their differences and relationships; but that is only an incident in the game. The typophil should gather around him those books which approximate most closely to his own conception of what a book should be. Some of them will find enjoyment not so much in tracking down the various characteristics of printing, be they beautiful or curious, healthy or morbid. The typophil will study the causes and the methods of these achievements, and in doing so he will not observe books alone, which are but a part of a realm which includes chapbooks and lectern Bibles, tram-tickets and posters, and the infinitude of ephemera created by the jobbing printer.[1] He will assemble printers' specimen books, histories of typography, treatises showing the descent of printing from script or letters carved in stone; he will be curious about the scholarship of printing, the theories and opinions of typographers, the confessions of printers, what triumphs and failures they have had, what difficulties they have surmounted, and how they have squared technique and vision.

The contemporary collector is fortunate, for in spite of the researches and discoveries of Stanley Morison the typographical seas are yet inadequately charted, and he may thus go forth not only in a spirit of adventure, but with high hope, for many of the secrets and treasures of printing, printers, and printeries still lie buried in places accessible to those who possess the spirit of the scholar or the investigator, without undue desire to intervene with the sport of the plutocratic collector.

1 See 'A Sanctuary of Printing' *infra*, pp. 251–264.

II

THE NONAGE OF NINETEENTH-CENTURY PRINTING IN ENGLAND

IT IS JUST AS ABSURD TO ASSUME THAT ALL THE PRINTING OF the good periods was good as it is to assume that all the printing of the bad periods was bad. Good periods, our own for instance, can, as we know, achieve a distinction in badness which might conceivably have made the worst printers of the bad periods say 'there, but for the grace of God, go we!' And the worst of it is that the worst typography of our own time is not the most primitive, but the most pretentious. There is a charm in naivety, so long as you do not get too much of it and, of course, so long as it is not a pose. One of the dangers of all periods of revival in art is the temptation to steal from the past rather than to learn from the past. In the art of typography the best printing of an age is not that which copies most successfully the most approved models of another age, but that which works within a convention peculiar and necessary to itself. Design in manufacture is adjustment to needs and, as every age has its own peculiar needs, good printing is that which fulfils them. It will be excellent as it is free from pose, preciosity, or mendacity.

This is a long preamble to a simple matter. But it is necessary, because I want to give a true perspective to what I have to say about a hitherto despised and rejected period of printing. It is all the more necessary because I am not advocating a revival of the characteristics, still less the methods, of that period. I am not alone in my weariness of those revivals which are merely epidemics of theft: 'period' printing is just as tedious as 'period' furniture and, ultimately, as worthless—with this difference: you may contrive to be comfortable in a mock Jacobean dining-room, but you cannot read with comfort the mock Gothic pages of a book even though it has been fabricated by a William Morris. 'Don't try to understand women,' said some one in one of Oscar Wilde's plays, 'look at them: women are pictures.' Books are not pictures. Books are made to be read and understood, and their typography must, without compromise of any kind, be in accordance with their primary object. Decadent printing is always ornamental printing. When typographical imagination fails it becomes decorative.

I write with all the authority of a convinced and unabashed reader of books and not as an expert in printing. There is a quality of typography which may be called readability. That quality is like manners in social life. It puts you at your ease in an atmosphere of welcome. It may be magnificent, but it does not draw your attention to its magnificence; it may be simple, but it does not draw your attention to its simplicity; it may even be monumental, but it must not be overpowering. It is conceivable that a test of good book-printing might be a rapid and appreciative merging of mind and book, with only a gradual realization that the volume was appropriately printed. This test applies, of course, mainly to books contrived for human nature's daily food: books that you are going to read. It does not rule out the showbook any more than the showdog negatives the agreeable, although not quite so highly bred, animal who flatters you on the slightest provocation by treating you as if you were a god. The showbook in the early stages of the printing revival of our own time served the excellent purpose of making an indifferent age aware of its typographical shortcomings. The best books produced as a result of that impulsion towards good printing are protests of beauty against ugliness rather than precepts and examples for ordinary practice. They bear much the same relation to books in general as monuments do to life in general. In the last resort they serve the same purpose as the table-books of Victorian days, but in a more exalted manner. One acclaims the beauty of the Kelmscott *Chaucer*, but one reads the father of English poetry in small pica and octavo. Nothing could be more appropriate then the Doves *Bible*. Its typographical austerity, its monumental simplicity, are the supreme compliment of the printing art to the chief treasury of our English tongue; but you would not read the Doves *Bible* even if you could afford to. Such books are monuments, homage to great authorship, and it is encouraging to feel that good printing has now come down to earth once more and is addressing itself successfully to the problem of making books which shall satisfy both the aesthetic sense and the need for utility.

The real progress of printing is an evolution from the complex to the simple, from the ornamental to the plain. There are masterpieces of both kinds. But the man who wants books to read, even though he keeps a few books for show, will turn most gratefully to those periods of printing which tend towards simple, plain, and friendly volumes. He will have special regard for the great times which threw up the smaller Aldines and Plantins and Elzevirs. He will regard with affection the lordly bookishness of the best typography of eighteenth-century England. He will turn, again, with gratitude to the Pickering period, and, if he is not a typographical prig, with real affection to the friendliness of the unpretentious printing of the first three decades of the nineteenth century.

It is a curious but not very important fact that typical eighteenth-century printing passed away with that century almost to the year. A mannered and formal age gave place to an age of conventional freedom. People began to wear their own hair and think their own thoughts. The tie wig and the panelled and ruled title-page passed away when the French Revolution got into its stride. *Lyrical Ballads*, though printed in 1792, was a trial piece of nineteenth-century typography, the characteristics of which still predominate. To realize the difference between the two styles it is only necessary to imagine the poems of Wordsworth in the format of, say, Pope, or even Gray. The difference would be something more than a difference of founts, type-faces, or page-building. The difference between the printing of the *Lyrical Ballads* and that of the *Elegy Written in a Country Churchyard* is the difference between one period and another, almost between two civilizations; certainly

POEMS,

BY

FELICIA DOROTHEA BROWNE.

LIVERPOOL:

PRINTED BY G. F. HARRIS,

FOR T. CADELL AND W. DAVIES, STRAND,

LONDON.

1808.

Title-page of Mrs. Hemans's first book. $11\frac{1}{4}'' \times 8\frac{3}{4}''$.

between two widely different expressions of the same civilization.

The typography of the first quarter of the nineteenth century has a special interest for us because we are still of the same period, if the tail end of it; for typographical changes are beginning to mark a new era. It marked the coming of a new reading public who were independent of a patrician class which had monopolized knowledge, largely by accident or tradition, just as it had monopolized so many other good things. Patronage was doomed, and writers had to win their way in the open market. Books began to be printed for everybody rather than for a cultured class and their scholarly dependents, on the one hand, and for an almost unlettered folk on the other. Thus we may note the passing of the noble 'library' quarto (as a century earlier we observed the dethronement of the even loftier folio) as well as of its opposite, the plebeian broadside and chapbook.

The books which took their places were for all classes. They lacked exclusiveness just as much as they lacked (to use the word for once in its proper sense) commonness. But they introduced a new element into book printing: a well-balanced familiarity free from pertness or shallowness, at once friendly and solid. Significantly the two main lines of evolution of this pre-Pickering period derive quite naturally from the two main traditions of the eighteenth century, from, on the one hand, the patrician austerity of fine printing which we associate with John Baskerville, Jacob Tonson, Bernard Lintot, and Robert Dodsley, and on the other

D

A

LOOKING-GLASS

FOR

The Ladies;

WHICH POSSESSES NOT ONLY THE PROPERTY OF

SHEWING

WHAT THEY ARE,

BUT

WHAT THEY OUGHT TO BE.

INTENDED

As a Companion to the "*Portraits of Fops;*" and
written by the same Author.

―――――――

" Look again. "

Shakespeare.

―――――――

LONDON:

PRINTED FOR AND PUBLISHED BY J. JOHNSTON, 98,
CHEAPSIDE.

―――

1812.

Title-page of *A Looking-Glass for the Ladies.* Actual size.

from the democratic chapbooks of the folk tradition. Neither, however, was the outcome of a pose or a fashion, and it is doubtful if any of the printers of the period were conscious of doing good printing, and still less were they desirous of fine printing. They just seem to have got on with their jobs, meeting the requirements of their times as well as they knew how.

The folk tradition may be traced in such books as *Broad Grins* by George Colman the Younger (1819). and *Poems* by Samuel Rogers (1814), both issued by Cadell & Davies, the former printed by M'Creery of Black Horse Court, and the latter by Bensley of Bolt Court. *Broad Grins* is a chapbook in improved circumstances replete with 'cuts' of a symbolical and humorous, though not too humorous, type; Rogers's *Poems*, as befits the works of our first plutocratic bard, is a super-chapbook ornamented with engravings by Clennell from drawings by T. Stothard, R.A.; it remains one of the most charming foolscap octavos of its period and one of the most satisfactory examples of the printing of verse. Another gratifying book of verse of the same time is Merivale's *Orlando in Roncesvalles* (1814), printed for John Murray by Richard and Arthur Taylor of Shoe Lane. Black-letters are used for the *canto* titles, and made to blend successfully with the romans of the tastefully built pages. Nearly all the major and much of the minor poetry of the period was well composed and printed within the new convention of the time. There are few more agreeable volumes than the first editions of Keats, Coleridge, Wordsworth, and some of Shelley, to name

ORLANDO

IN

RONCESVALLES,

𝔄 𝔓𝔬𝔢𝔪,

IN FIVE CANTOS.

BY

J. H. MERIVALE, Esq.

ALERE FLAMMAM.

LONDON:

PRINTED FOR JOHN MURRAY,

50, ALBEMARLE STREET,

BY RICHARD AND ARTHUR TAYLOR, SHOE-LANE.

1814.

Title-page of Merivale's *Orlando in Roncesvalles.* 7¾″×5″.

Poems,

BY

JOHN KEATS.

" What more felicity can fall to creature,
" Than to enjoy delight with liberty."

Fate of the Butterfly.—SPENSER.

LONDON:

PRINTED FOR

C. & J. OLLIER, 3, WELBECK STREET,

CAVENDISH SQUARE.

1817.

Title-page of first edition of Keats's *Poems*. Actual size.

but a few famous poets then looked upon as intruders. The early Scotts, both prose and verse, were admirable also in their way, but they were printed at one of the great printing offices with an established reputation. I prefer to base my evidence of the virtues of the period on the work of the minor offices. The reader who desires to pursue this class of poetry printing should keep an eye on the obscure printer. He will find many treasures. The thirteenth edition of Charles Cotton's *Scarronides*, printed in the chapbook style by J. Galton of Little Eastcheap in 1804, and *Rejected Odes*, edited by Humphrey Hedgehog, Esq. (1813), printed by Hamblin & Seyfang, Garlick Hill, are two examples. Better-known printers have innumerable examples. The *Craniad* (1817), printed by James Ballantyne, is a favourite of mine, and a library could be made from the pleasantly printed volumes of the Whittingham offices, even before the days of Pickering; and at the dawn of the Pickering era, from the books printed by Whittingham for Samuel Weller Singer, among the best of them being George Chapman's *Hymns of Homer* (1838), which has some of the self-consciousness of fine printing.

To come again within the limits of the nonage of nineteenth-century printing, there are the early books of Southey, particularly *Omniana* (1812), a 12mo in two volumes, printed by W. Pople of Chancery Lane. The friendly characteristics of these pleasant volumes are everywhere in evidence. The edition of Miss Collier's *Art of Tormenting* (1806), with its frontispiece by Gillray, is a good example. It was, however, printed by William

PROMETHEUS UNBOUND

A LYRICAL DRAMA

IN FOUR ACTS

WITH OTHER POEMS

BY

PERCY BYSSHE SHELLEY

AUDISNE HÆC, AMPHIARAE, SUB TERRAM ABDITE?

LONDON
C AND J OLLIER VERE STREET BOND STREET
1820

Title-page of first edition of Shelley's *Prometheus Unbound.* $8\frac{1}{4}'' \times 5\frac{3}{4}''$.

Bulmer, who only belongs to a nonage by accident of birth. Many of the theological books of those years were well done. There is a fine example in *The New Week's Preparation for a Worthy Receiving of the Lord's Supper* (1811), which recalls the preceding era of typography. And it must not be forgotten that provincial offices, often in remote places, were turning out work which was not only in character with the age but equal to the best that was being done in London.

As time went on, the friendly printing of this period passed first into the printing inspired by William Pickering after the Aldines, and its real character ended with the books published by Moxon, and the Victorian table-books of the fifties and sixties. Then came chaos and decadence in types, imposition, ornaments, paper, and binding. The Pre-Raphaelites began the revival. From them came Morris, who flirted first with the Caslon founts, and then, 'scrapping the lot', he started a new era of printing with new type-faces grafted on to the oldest models. He threw back to the primitive, and thus gave us a new start, but neither he nor his followers have produced typography which you should do more than admire and pass by. The books of the early eighteen-hundreds were rarely monumental, they were friendly and stimulated that sort of affection which is appropriate to a communion with books.

III

PRINTING & FINE PRINTING

PRINTING BEING HUMAN CAN BE GOOD OR BAD; BUT THE victory and its rewards do not always go to the best, or to the worst, but to the middling sort. Yet the best printing, even when it seems to be ineffectual, is a preservative. Even the worst printing is ultimately innocuous because if let alone it cures by killing itself. Decadence is disintegration. The trouble is with the smug average, the pervasive So-So! 'So-so is good, very excellent good, and yet 'tis not, 'tis but so-so!' A creaking gate hangs longest, and mediocrity in printing is a long time dying, if it ever dies. There is always an uncritical demand, and to those who profit by that demand so-so is good, very excellent good; and there are plenty of business reasons for leaving well alone. Yet it is dangerous to leave well alone. Dangerous to the condition called 'well', because if it is left alone it becomes ill. For ultimate well-being it does not matter because, in the lag between bad and good, cells or nuclei of discontent are developed among people of taste or goodwill. Dissatisfaction with bad conditions may take the form of an exaggerated desire for perfection. Aesthetic starvation, for instance, produces beauty-worship as surely as a starved social consciousness produces utopianism. In printing, an undernourished typographical system provokes visions of Fine Printing, Ideal Books, and Books Beautiful. The private presses of the eighteen-nineties were protests against bad printing.

E

But although idealism may be a malady, utopian dreams have their advantages, even in printing. The example of the utopist has more than once saved printing from complete degradation. On the other hand, Fine Printing can be misleading, wasteful, and finally useless, especially in the hands of the commercially minded, and more particularly when the commercial mind is tainted with a sentimental passion for handicraft. Thus the Kelmscott Press found its nemesis in Elbert Hubbard's Roycroft Books.

How far the typographical idealist should be allowed to go is a matter of opinion—and demand. There is, indeed, much to be said for idealism as experimentation and, so long as the principles of typography are understood and respected, there can be no ultimate harm in *éditions de luxe* and when a book is a work of art the appreciation of it cannot go too far. The statement that it may be a work of art will not pass unchallenged, nor should it, for a book is on the borderline. Experts, as usual, disagree, and opinions are further confused by interests and sentiments, both notorious trespassers upon good judgement.

A book, or rather a 'fine book', according to Paul Valéry, is both a 'perfect reading device' and a 'work of art'. It is a work of art because it has a personality of its own, bearing the marks of special thought and suggesting 'the noble intention of a happy and free arrangement'. But the path of creative printing is not smooth, for 'typography excludes improvization', yet personality will have its way.

'The mind of the writer', he says, 'is seen as in a mirror which the printing press provides. If the paper and the ink are in accord, if the type is clear, if the composition is well looked after, the adjustment of line perfect, and the sheet well printed, the author feels his language and his style anew. He thinks he hears a clearer, firmer voice than his own, a voice faultlessly pure, articulating his words, dangerously detaching all his words. Everything feeble, effeminate, arbitrary, and inelegant which he wrote, speaks too clearly and too loud. To be magnificently printed is a very precious and important tribute.'[1]

When Charles Lamb, having, it is said, done all he could to the manuscript of an essay, sent it to press with the exclamation: 'It's the print that does it!' he was thinking of printing as an aid to his own expression and not as an art in itself, and it is conceivable that he would have resented any attempt on the part of the printer or typographer to represent Elia other than as he was in the eyes of Elia's creator, namely, himself. But, on the other hand, we can imagine a writer of feeble, effeminate, or inelegant stuff enjoying, without of course admitting, the sublimation of his work by printer or typographer. That, however, is not the aim or the basis of the art of printing, in so far as printing is an art, although it is one of the risks. The words 'fine' and 'printing' are dangerous bedfellows, for they are apt to beget monstrosities. Good printing, like poetry in Keats's opinion, should be unobtrusive, 'a thing which enters into one's soul, and does not startle or amaze it with itself, but with its subject'.

Printing and writing have more than the obvious

1 Trans. Theodore W. Koch. Quoted in *The Ideal Book*, ed. Peter Garnett, The Laboratory Press, Pittsburg (1934).

relationship of lines of communication. They are both allied with talking. The printer multiplies or extends the talk of the writer, and since writing, whether prose or poetry, has sound as well as sense, the preservation of its cadences is essential. If, therefore, the human voice sounds through the written word it should carry also through the printed word. It is the writer who sets the pace because without him there would be nothing to print, and as writing is the first substitute for talking it is necessary to unequivocal expression that the voice of the writer should not be obliterated. The voice is in the words. Printing transmits them. Transmission is a delicate and responsible art, for it translates into a new medium something that has already been translated from the brain of an author into writing. The reader does not want to see the printer but to hear the writer. Fine, fancy, or ostentatious printing may thus be something more than bad taste: it may be disrespectful to the author and offensive to the reader.

Whether printing has an independent art-life is not an easy problem to solve since there is no generally acceptable definition of a work of art. We all, whether critics or laymen, think we know a work of art when we see one; but even after making allowances for differences of taste, prejudice, and whim, which do not affect the general proposition, the right of admission into the palace of art is subject to fantastic fluctuations. Poetry is an art, but literary history reveals that a poet may please some critics all the time and all critics some of the time, but not all critics all the time. Pope at one

time was believed to be a poet and an artist. Later critics
(some of them poets as well) called him an artist, but
refused to admit him into the hierarchy of the poets.
Contemporary criticism would seem to swing him back
on to his poetic pedestal. The only one who is indifferent to these mutations is the poet himself. Labels and
arguments do not in the long run affect him. He may look
on and smile 'from his abode where the eternal are', or,
if he is still living, he goes on writing what he believes
to be poetry and the common reader goes on reading it
regardless, or amusedly regardful, of critics and criticism. It is the same with printing; whether it is an art
or not is a secondary affair, so long as it is good printing.
'Art happens', says Whistler, and the printer who sets
out to be an artist is liable to make a mess of both art
and print.

There are those who argue that printing is sometimes
an art and sometimes something else: a craft, for instance,
craftsmanship being the snobbism for something supposed to be superior to a piece of machine made merchandise. A brief examination of the problem from this
aspect may prove more fruitful for, although the status
of a work of art may be higher or lower in the scale of
critical opinion, merchandise can be measured for its
utility. But although some, like Eric Gill, argue that
there is no fundamental difference between a work of
art and a useful piece of goods, an uneasy division exists
between the useful arts and the fine arts. Their frontiers
are still loosely defined. The wits of the eighteen-
nineties would not allow the fine arts (which for them

were the only arts) to be useful and beautiful at one and
the same time. They believed that the business of art
was to be beautiful. We now suspect that to be nonsense, just as we no longer believe that it is the business
of art to hold the mirror up to nature. Art can be
beautiful and it does, on occasion, reflect nature, even as
that term is popularly understood. But, on the other
hand, it can be ugly and it can and does distort and defy
nature, whilst at the same time and in its own way
remaining a part of that nature it is supposed to reflect.

Printing has the same peculiarities. A printed page
can be so beautiful that you would rather frame it than
read it, and it can be so ugly that it is not only difficult
but nauseating to read. Yet the object of a book is to
be read, not merely looked at, and any printing which
directly or indirectly, deliberately or accidentally, de-
tracts from the primary and fundamental purpose is bad
printing. Bad printing is not always mediocre or incompetent printing, it is often what is called 'fine printing'.
The phrase is unfortunate because it is inexact and can,
therefore, be twisted by the mercenary as well as by the
aesthetical to accommodate their own wishes. But when
we speak of the 'fine arts', although we are using an
inexact term, we know what we are talking about and
everybody else knows what we are talking about. We
mean the useless as distinct from the useful arts. We
mean poems, statues, pictures, symphonies, not pots and
pans, frocks, gardens, houses, ships, and bridges. We do
not generally mean printing, although the 'fine book',
especially when it is superfine, a masterpiece by say

Didot bound by Dérome, or the Kelmscott *Chaucer* in pigskin by Cobden-Sanderson, or Baskerville's *Shaftesbury* in the red morocco of Roger Payne, has been raised to the peerage of the fine arts. The 'fine arts' are definite: they are the patrician arts. The term is a survival from a period when one small class was content to surround itself with beautiful things as a means of escape from a distasteful environment, without any desire to impose its tastes or standards upon outsiders. The 'fine book' belongs to that period, and has nothing to do with the cradle-days of printing. It became an anachronism after 1789. The 'fine books' of our time, however modern, are equally anachronistic.[1]

The chief fault of the amateur printers of the eighteen-nineties was that they were not content to be printers. They wished to be artistic printers, and the situation was complicated by the belief that art was mainly concerned with the creation of beauty, and beauty in turn was largely a matter of decoration. They had a morbid suspicion of monotony and avoided simple patterns and plain textures, never realizing that whatever happens to printing the alternatives to most of its operations make for adequate variety.[2] Thus when they came to make a

[1] I know that an anachronism in art or craft may be interesting, or in modern jargon, amusing—but that is another story. [2] For the benefit of the lay reader of this book it may be noted that the typographer has ample margin for the exercise of taste and ingenuity in the following operations without resort to extraneous ornamentation: size of page, disposition of margins, headlines, capitals, italics, footnotes &c.; choice of types, paper, binding materials; design and lettering of cover; arrangement of title and other preliminary pages; disposition of contents, index, and colophon and other machinery of a book, and, if any, illustrations; and finally the character of the end papers.

book they insisted upon making it beautiful and they succeeded so well that what after all is a tool for reading was often sacrificed to its looks. It was as though a modern armament manufacturer suddenly threw back to decorated muskets and swords, or a tool maker began to ornament his hammers and chisels. Such results are surprising because the artist-printers revived, perhaps even invented, the idea that a book was not merely a device for holding together a number of printed pages but, as Charles Ricketts defined it, 'an aggregate of living parts harmoniously controlled',[1] or, in matter-of-fact language, an assembly of paper, ink, binding, and type in an agreeable as well as a convenient design.

This respect for co-ordination was deep-rooted in the men of the period. It was their faith. Even so earnest an advocate of the Book Beautiful as T. J. Cobden-Sanderson, who in association with Emery Walker took the first steps towards lifting the designing of books out of the medieval convention revived by Morris, makes a distinction between typography and beautiful typography. 'The whole duty of Typography, as of Calligraphy', he says, 'is to communicate to the imagination, without loss by the way, the thought or image intended to be communicated by the Author. That definition may well have inspired recent good printing as well as the self-conscious books of the Doves Press.[2] Cobden-Sanderson went on to say that:

'The whole duty of beautiful typography is not to substitute

1 *A Bibliography of the Books by Hacon and Ricketts* (1904), by Charles Ricketts, Introd. 7–9.   2 See Notes, p. 268, *infra*.

for the beauty or interest of the thing thought and intended to be conveyed by the symbol, a beauty or interest of its own, but, on the one hand, to win access for that communication by the clearness and beauty of the vehicle, and on the other hand, to take advantage of every pause or stage in that communication to interpose some characteristic and restful beauty in its own art. We thus have a reason for the clearness and beauty of the text as a whole, for the especial beauty of the first or introductory page and of the title, and for the especial beauty of the headings of chapters, capital or initial letters, and so on, and an opening for the illustrator. . . .'[1]

And he concludes by charging with treason those who depart from the true faith by permitting 'the self-assertion of any Art beyond the limits imposed by the conditions of its service'.

It was not, however, the typography but the building of the book which was the real contribution to what has been called the 'Revival of Printing'. And it was appropriate and perhaps inevitable that a new attitude towards the designing of books should have come out of the Arts and Crafts Movement, for that movement sought to abolish the division of labour and to restore the organic character of the useful arts.

The complete abolition of the division of labour was not achieved, for although William Morris became a printer he was never a binder and was forced to delegate most of the operations in the construction of the Kelmscott books. But he retained control of the whole job and thus prepared the way for the modern typographer[2] who stands in the same relation to a book as the architect

1 *Ecce Mundus: Industrial Ideals and the Book Beautiful* (1902).   2 See Notes, p. 269, *infra*.

stands towards a building. 'No art is nearer to architecture than typography', says Henri Focillon, Director
of the Musée de Lyon; 'like architecture, its first principle is the discriminative and proper adaptation of
materials. Like architecture, it rests upon a system of
definite conclusions. Its economies are fixed, it repudiates contorted eccentricities. As the designer of a palace
cunningly distributes shadows and light on his façade
and, in the plans of interiors, adjusts light and shade to
living needs, so the designer of a book employs two
contrasting qualities, the white of the paper and the
black of the ink, assigns to each its part and attains a
harmonious whole. There are in architecture great
calm planes that are comparable to the margins of a
page. There are in a book symmetries and modulations like those of a building. Indeed, is it not true that
these two great works of man, a book and a house,
should aim at the same fundamental virtue—style? I
mean rightness, soberness without sadness, majesty
without exaggeration, combined with a personal touch
and a noble charm which completely satisfy the spirit.'[1]

The modern typographer may have as little practical
experience of printing as the architect of masonry, but
he has done more for the craft of printing in the last
twenty years than the best of the practical printers in
the preceding three hundred years. Morris might have
been shocked but he would have approved, for in spite
of mechanization the 'human element' in printing has

---

[1] Quoted from Introd. to *Le Livre, son architecture, sa technique*, by
Marius Audin (Lyons, 1924), in *The Fine Book* (1934), 56-7.

not been entirely eliminated. It has survived even mechanical composing. The compositor remains the mason of typography, and type-setting in its mechanical form is still a craft like bricklaying; for the printer, as William Morris and Emery Walker pointed out in the first collection of *Arts and Crafts Essays* (1893), is engaged not only in laying the type in a workmanlike manner, but in giving it a balanced appearance by breaking up lines and 'rivers' 'as in bonding masonry or brick work.' Neither types nor bricks can be well and truly laid unless they achieve these aims.

Charles Ricketts, who helped to restore a 'sense of design' to book production, rightly claimed novelty for the Kelmscott and Vale books because by reviving that sense, in addition to restoring the 'element of personal control', it became possible, 'for the first time in the history of printing', to master all the operations which go to the making of a book. There can be little doubt, as Ricketts continues, 'that the invention of the type and the original woodcut pictures and decorations form an aggregate for which we will hardly find a precedent in the past', and that 'the control of the pagination and press-work has very rarely been due in the past to the designer of the type and the rest'. Of all the lessons of the 'private presses' there can now be little doubt that the control of the whole book in a consistent design is the most important, and has had the greatest influence on modern typography and book production.

Theories, however logical, may conflict with practice, however sincere. This conflict is obvious in the Vale

Press books. Ricketts, striving for the co-ordination of exquisite parts, ends by exploiting the exquisite. He believes in packing a book with beauty inside and out. A book should not only be 'alive in every part' but 'definite' and even 'emphatic' in design. In the past, however, the parts of a book were not expected to show off; they were expected to be of good report, and not to brag about it. During the greater part of last century a well-designed book was so rare that self-consciousness in the early days of the revival was inevitable and even excusable. All would have been well if the precursors of a new typography had been inimitable. But they were far from that, and they increased and multiplied, legitimately and illegitimately. A craftsman's dream, splendid in itself, became a racket. There is an ostentation about many of the fine books of the nineties and those of our own time which makes them more attractive to collectors than to readers or scholars. They are so obviously well-dressed that even their creators sometimes resort to explaining or defending them. The admission that such books are not for everyday use is sufficient condemnation.

'The aim of the revival of printing', says Ricketts, 'is . . . merely due to a wish to give a permanent and beautiful form to that portion of our literature which is secure of permanence. By a permanent form I do not mean merely sound as to paper and ink, etc.; I mean permanent in the sense that the work reflects that conscious aim towards beauty and order which are ever interesting elements in themselves.'[1]

1 *A Bibliography of the Books issued by Hacon and Ricketts* (1904), by Charles Ricketts, Introd. 16.

The curious thing is that both Ricketts and Morris in addition to the work of their presses produced or designed good books by ordinary trade and mechanical methods, but so obsessed were they with art and handicraft that neither of them seems to have realized the possibilities of the beneficent example they had thus set before all printers. Yet printing as we know it to-day, although indirectly stimulated by the example of the Kelmscott and Vale books, follows the 'trade' productions and not the 'artistic' books of the private presses. The progenitors of modern printing are the *Roots of the Mountains* and *Daphnis and Chloe* rather than the Vale *Shakespeare* and the Kelmscott *Chaucer*.[1] The creations of the private presses of the nineties have come to occupy the ironical position of being little more than sublimations of what John Johnson calls the 'lively, if ill-defined, archaism which swept over the country in the second half of Victoria's reign'.[2]

There must always be room for the hand-made book, and that room may possibly expand as standardization increases its grip upon our works and lives. But beautiful books are no longer dependent upon the handicraftsman. Books of fine quality and individual distinction are now produced by mechanical methods and, although they differ from the hand-made books, they have a character and charm of their own and they serve the

1 I have touched upon this theme in the chapter on 'The Revival of Printing' in *The Eighteen Nineties* (1913), now published in Cape's 'Life and Letters Series', and A. J. A. Symons has dealt more fully with it in his essay on 'The Typography of the 'Nineties', *The Fleuron*, vii (1930).
2 *The Printer, his Customers, and his Men*, by John Johnson (1933), 31.

purposes of a book as well as their predecessors did and much better than many of·the hand-made books of yesterday and to-day. The contemporary range of well-designed books of the common kind is also wider and more varied, and the non-critical reader gets better printing to-day whether he wants it or not. It is wrong to assume, as some do, that the rank and file of readers for whom standardized and mass-produced books exist have been seduced by traders from appreciating 'quality'. The casual reader has no recognizable taste for quality in printing, and when all books were hand made the proletariat could not read and the middle class as we know it did not exist:

> *Book-larning* hereabouts is rarish:
> I'm thought a *schollard* in my parish.
> For in the village where I dwell,
> Not one can read, and few can spell.[1]

Ruskin was the first English author to offer working men good printing—at a price beyond their reach—and up to his death only those few who became Socialists or who came under the influence of the University Settlement Movement paid any attention to him. Then his greatest disciple Morris had another shot and produced the Kelmscott masterpieces for millionaires. It is the commercial typographer of to-day who has broken through the ring of badness and is forcing traders and machines to do their best rather than their worst. For

1 Rev. John Horseman, Rector of Heydon, 1811. Quoted T. F. Dibdin, *Literary Reminiscences* (1836), i. 301.

proof of this it is only necessary to turn to the excellent design of contemporary series of popular reprints.[1]

Few things are so misleading as historical analogy. To argue that the people of this or that period did so and so and that therefore the people of this should do the same is nonsense. It is a kind of nonsense favoured by those who advocate a return to handicraft. There is little or no resemblance between the people of the handicraft age and those of the machine age. The people of to-day who have no interest in how a thing is made but a great deal in how to get enough of it are so different from their predecessors that they might be an entirely new race. They and the conditions under which they live exist now for the first time. Machines are their gods and the product of machines their treasure. Indeed, they themselves are products of mechanization, and they not only prefer, but, in the circumstances, it is perhaps natural that they should prefer, to be led by gadgets rather than by ideas.

Hand-press work is not excellent in itself, as anybody knows who has studied the publications of the seventeenth and late eighteenth centuries. There are black

[1] Pocketable reprints have generally shown a typographical taste and ingenuity. It began with the smaller Elzevirs and Plantins and has not yet ended: on the contrary, the publication of such admirably designed series as the *Temple Classics, Temple Shakespeare, Temple Bible*, the *Phoenix*, the *Travellers Library*, the *Florin Books*, Constable's *Miscellany*, and the *Penguin Books,* to name but a few in England, and the *Albatross* (a masterpiece of typography, more satisfying to my taste than any *édition de luxe*), the new *Tauchnitz*, and the so-called Inselbücherei, a series produced by the Insel-Verlag in Leipzig, at a price of 0,70 RM.=about 9d., most beautifully printed, often illustrated, and widely circulated in Germany, shows that good printing is no handicap to circulation.

sheep also among black letters. Bad printing is bad whether it has been set and printed by hand or set and printed by machine. Most of the characteristics of the two methods are the same. The few differences, such for instance as texture, are accidental. Worship of the irregularities of hand work is sentimental. There would have been fewer irregularities if the printer could have avoided them. What makes printing good is neither the ritualism of handicraft nor the methodism of the machine, but the accordance of the design with the wishes of the reader who wants to get down to the business of reading. Good printing is readable printing, and no print is readable that is not simple, direct, plain, and inclining towards austerity. Printing is not a thing in itself like a picture, admitting the maximum of personal expression, but part of a tool called a book: a bridge between writer and reader. It should contain nothing to impede that traffic. Graciousness, friendliness, even dignity should be there, but always unobtrusively. Self-effacement is the etiquette of the good printer.

PART II

THE AUTHOR & HIS PRINTER

I

AUTHORS & PRINTING

THE APATHY OF THE MAJORITY OF AUTHORS TOWARDS THE aesthetics of book production is one of the more curious phenomena of print-lore. Some observers think the author is indifferent, but Bernard Shaw believes 'it is quite a mistake to think that the author is merely insensible to the beauty of a finely designed and well-printed page; he positively hates it'. There is still another explanation: I would suggest that the typographical tolerance of the author is due not to indifference, insensibility, or hatred, but to conceit. The typographical sense of the average author is sacrificed to the desire of print at any cost. It is not printing but getting into print that matters:

> 'Tis pleasant, sure, to see one's name in print;
> A book's a book, although there's nothing in't.[1]

Ruskin was always a little uneasy about printing because he thought it tended to encourage a morbid desire for publicity. In *Fors Clavigera* he refers to 'the invention of printing, and the easy power and extreme pleasure to vain persons of seeing themselves in print'. The obsession might be bad for printing if there were neither publishing houses with respectable traditions nor adventurous typographers who have made good printing accessible to all. As it is, and particularly at the present time, there is no cause for alarm; for although the

[1] Byron, *English Bards and Scotch Reviewers* (1809).

printer may take the line of least resistance and print anything that does not break the laws against libel and obscenity, in any style or absence of style the author will tolerate, there are publishers who know how to take care of the typographically careless author.

On the other hand, there have always been authors who believe that responsibility to their readers does not end until the written word is given more than a chance setting. These writers have done something towards restoring the sort of harmony between printer and publisher which may have existed before printing and publishing were divorced, for they have helped to preserve good taste during periods of apathy or degeneration, by adding to the technique of the printer what Falconer Madan called those 'personal touches which confer distinction on a book, and transform a mere well-arranged contact of ink and paper under the guidance of machinery into a treasure for all time'.[1]

If any party to this dispute hates a well-printed page it is the printer. This notion is supported in modern times by the behaviour of authors who happen to have been printers, or connected by family with printers. No outstanding example of printing, for instance, is associated with the names of Benjamin Franklin in America or William Cobbett in England, and examples could be multiplied. Walt Whitman was a printer in his youth, but he did not dream of inventing a new typography to go with his new poetry. Samuel Richardson was a printer who became a novelist as well, but no one ever

[1] *The Daniel Press* (Oxford, 1921), 47.

thinks of a Richardson style of printing although he printed his own novels. Mark Twain was once a printer, but you could not tell it from his editions, which are no better and no worse than the average commercial stuff. William Dean Howells was born in the printing-office of a country paper in Ohio and could not 'breathe the familiar odour of types and presses without emotion'. He notes with appreciation that 'the printers of that day had nearly all some affinity with literature, if not some love of it'. In his father's printing-office he says, 'we enjoyed our trade as the decorative art it also is. Questions of taste constantly arose . . . they did not go far . . . but they employed the critical faculty and aesthetic instinct, and they allied us, however slightly and unconsciously, with the creators of the beautiful.' All of which is excellent, and it is good also to be told that the novelist himself was responsible for maintaining a quiet dignity in the advertising pages of the family paper. 'I am rather proud, in my quality of printer, that this was the style which I established; and we maintained it against all advertisers, who then as now wished to outshriek one another in large type and ugly woodcuts.'[1] But Howell's influence on printing went no farther and, as we know, it did not last.

The restoration of design in printing and book-production was not, in fact, inspired by the professional printer but by two scholarly amateurs of printing. They were the Rev. C. H. O. Daniel, Warden of Worcester

[1] *The Country Printer: an Essay*. William Dean Howells. Privately Printed. [N.D.]

College, Oxford, and William Morris, poet and Admirable Crichton of the Arts and Crafts Movement. Daniel became a printer to please himself and his friends, and Morris to reform a craft by reviving respect for quality in design, technique, and materials. Each of them achieved distinction and a certain modernity in spite of a deliberate antiquarianism.

The important point, however, is that the modern revival of printing was forced upon the printing-office from without by men who were neither printers nor, primarily, business men; and even when a business man has preserved or supported good taste in printing he has usually been a publisher rather than a printer. William Pickering saved printing from complete degeneracy in the middle of last century. Geoffrey Keynes, in his monograph on that publisher, says, 'commercial book-production at the present time owes more to Pickering's enterprise than has ever been either claimed or admitted'. It was the great printer-publishers Jacob Tonson, Bernard Lintot, and Robert Dodsley who gave beauty and style to eighteenth-century printing, just as it was publishers like Pickering, Moxon, Field & Tuer, Elkin Mathews, John Lane, and J. M. Dent who by their example in the nineteenth century helped to defend printing from printers who were content to do as they were told, and, if no one told them, to follow rule-of-thumb methods which tended always to become worse rather than better. There were, of course, other forces at work, mainly commercial, but they need not detain us, for it is not denied that the 'revival

of printing' of the nineties received its initial stimulus from the presses of the amateurs. I say 'stimulus'
because the tradition of good printing had never really
been lost. It had been preserved by the two University
presses, and by certain printers in London and Edinburgh; as well as by those few publishers who followed
the example of Pickering and Moxon; whilst others
had even ventured to break through the uniformity
of the better class of contemporary printing by making a harmony or design of a whole book. In many
instances the formats thus created were superior to the
printing. It was the publisher, however, not the printer,
who first took up the cause, and the idea that the writer
could influence either printer or publisher was rarely
considered.

It was long before the average printer took advantage
of the awakening of typographical taste which began in
the eighteen-nineties.[1] The men who extended and con-
solidated that taste came from anywhere but the printing-
offices. The majority of modern typographers are intel-
lectuals or scholars who have forced themselves upon
the trade, generally through the publishing houses.
There was probably some resistance to their efforts, for
as recently as 1927 Stanley Morison was advocating
'a greater degree of co-operation between printer and

[1] The revival of printing in the eighteen-nineties was the result of
dissatisfaction which had been going on for some time. In 1882 Henry
Stevens of Vermont read a paper before the Library Association at Cambridge, in which he analysed, under the title *Who Spoils our New English
Books,* the causes of the decay of printing, and came to much the same
conclusions as those which moved Morris to action nearly ten years later.
See Notes, pp. 270–1, *infra.*

publisher' in order to raise the 'general level of book production'. He left the maintenance of the 'level of publishing' to the influence of the 'reading and writing classes',[1] ignoring the possibility of their influencing printing as well.

It is not often that writers express opinions upon printing, but it happens that in the same year, and at a time when monumental copies and all manner of freaks in Large Paper were rampant, a distinguished poet, Walter de la Mare, was very properly on the side of the angels in the precincts of the Double Crown Club.

'Unless', he said, 'a book is to be a museum piece it must be fit for instant and widespread service, and not too dainty for human thumbs and human usage. . . . It is something of a mystery who buys limited and expensive editions of books—since men of taste are seldom greedy of publicity; but it is even more of a mystery who reads in them.[2] On the other hand, a thumbed and battered copy of even the most ornate and expensive of books will for every new reader in turn confer a pleasure all its own.'[3]

There is room for criticism of the pioneer books of the modern presses but, pretentious as many of them are, the best of them have added to a 'well-arranged contact of ink and paper' qualities of character and good taste.

1 Stanley Morison, *A Review of Recent Typography in England, the United States, France, and Germany* (1927), 5.   2 A similar opinion was more emphatically expressed at about the same time by D. H. Lawrence: 'How mad people are—there is quite a large vogue in editions de luxe that cost two or five or even twenty-five pounds.   I hate it.'   Quoted, Frieda Lawrence in *Not I, but the Wind . . .* (1935), 25.   3 *The Printing of Poetry*, a Paper read before the Double Crown Club, Feb. 12th, 1931, by Walter de la Mare (Printed for the Club at the University Press, Cambridge, by Walter Lewis, 1931), 29–30.

Such an achievement would justify the inference that still more benefits may follow, not necessarily in the limited field of the private press or its imitators, but by an intensified demand for good taste in common printing.

The writer and the printer have so much in common as to suggest an inevitable partnership in taste. The one could not get along very well without the other, and although authors sometimes become their own printers, they rarely do so from choice. Every author knows that the main body of printing, whether in good or bad taste, must come through what are known as trade channels and be subjected to the risks of trial and error common to all workmanship, as well as to the handicaps of commercial production, for which nowadays there is less excuse than there used to be. These reasons indicate that a pragmatical alliance between writers and printers might be of common advantage, provided, of course, that taste and inventiveness on the part of the author were added to the presumed technical competence of the printer. No good purpose could be served by the mere contact of a typographically ignorant or tasteless author and an incompetent printer, any more than good could follow from the petty interferences of an ill-informed author with a printer who knew his job.

In the past, associations of the kind, whether good or bad, were infrequent and, whilst the annals of literature abound with references to the drudgery of proof-reading and the pitfalls of publishing, few authors other than those directly interested in typography refer to the aesthetics of printing. But when the letters and diaries of the present time are published more references of the kind should appear, for writers as a class no longer take the printing of their books for granted. Inspired, no doubt, by the general quickening of typographical taste, they are prepared to encourage experiments and even to have opinions of their own. Exhibitions of printing and the annual selection of the 'Fifty Best Books', in England by the First Edition Club, and in America by the Grolier Club, are making authors 'type-conscious'. And finally, the researches of Stanley Morison[1] are providing a fund of knowledge which should help to keep printers on the rails for at least a century to come.

Daniel and Morris were the first disturbers of the bad old peace, for without the example of their presses the modern impulsion towards good printing must have been seriously delayed. The awakening was at first slow, and sometimes misguided, but the later results have been solid, especially where the motives rather than the methods of the masters have been copied. Daniel and Morris were revivalists, and their typography suffers from the over-emphasis inseparable from revivalist conditions, whether aesthetic or religious. But, although their followers have frequently produced 'period furniture', the leaders blew the breath of life into an old technique by adding something personal and organic and thus escaping the perils of tradition-mongering.

They were preceded by Horace Walpole and Sir

[1] 'The greatest figure in the history of the last three centuries of the printing craft.' John Johnson, Printer to the University of Oxford, *The Printer, his Customers, and his Men* (1933), 50.

Egerton Brydges, both of whom had their own 'private' presses, managed for them by skilled printers at Strawberry Hill (1757–89) and Lee Priory (1813–22). Those presses were probably the first links in this country between the enthusiasm of the amateur of books and the craft of printing. Walpole hopes 'future edition-mongers' will say that 'those of Strawberry Hill' have 'all the beautiful negligence of a gentleman'. He admitted no purpose but his own amusement; at the same time, the Strawberry Hill publications prove that his amusement was far from being entirely frivolous or modish. Egerton Brydges made no such claim but, being a bibliophile with a keen sense of rarity, he doubtless got a considerable amount of fun out of his very limited and often learned editions.

Other amateurs had toyed no doubt with the idea of becoming printers and there are records of two distinguished poets going further. William Cowper tried his hand at printing, apparently without very much success. He hoped to 'proceed even to the printing of Halfpenny Ballads' but decided ultimately 'to employ', he told his sister, 'an ingenious mechanic of the town to make me a longer case; for you may observe that my lines turn up their tails like Dutch mastiffs, so difficult do I find it to make the two halves exactly coincide with the other'.[1] William Blake is in a class by himself. He was an engraver by trade and designed formats for his own works which he executed himself without the aid of typography by a process of engraving not yet fully

1 *Correspondence of William Cowper*, ed. Thomas Wright (1914), ii, p. 7.

understood. Those works, although unappreciated in his time except by the 'acute but honourable minority', are highly valued to-day for their originality in crafts-manship and artistry.

I am here concerned with the influence of the author rather than with that of the amateur of printing, and upon the professional rather than the amateur trend of the craft; and if even those authors who appreciate good printing have been content to play the part of guests at the banquet a minority, not confined to our own time, have insisted upon having a finger in the printers' pie. There is internal evidence that even in the seventeenth century there were authors, like Robert Burton, writer of the *Anatomy of Melancholy*,[1] who had typographical taste, and earlier in that century Sir Henry Savile, Bodley's friend and co-founder of the Oxford library, was probably the first author to procure types for his own use. John Evelyn laments, in a letter to Samuel Pepys, the loss of 'those elegant types of Sir Henry Savile's, at Eton, which that learned knight procured with great cost for his edition of *St. Chrysostom*'.

In the eighteenth century the high standard of culture among the patricians was reflected in printing so that neither the curious nor the elegant writer had cause for anxiety about the presentation of his works. Laurence Sterne, who was not an amateur typographer, is con-scious of the high standards of printing among reputable publishers, for when he offers *Tristram Shandy* to Dodsley he proposes 'to print a lean edition, in two small volumes,

1 See Notes, pp. 271-2, *infra*.

of the size of *Rasselas'*, not only at his own expense, 'merely to feel the pulse of the world', but 'in so creditable a way as to paper, type, &c., as to do no dishonour to you, who, I know, never chuse to print a book meanly'.[1] It is not known whether the first instalments of the first edition were printed in York or in London, although it is believed that Sterne inclined to a local printer, probably Ann Ward, widow of Caesar Ward, at the Sign of the Bible, in Coney Street, 'with whose neat and accurate typography', says Robert Davies, the antiquary, 'the author was well acquainted'. The 'neat and accurate typography' of *Tristram Shandy* in a friendly and pocketable format which had all the charm and none of the hauteur of the larger formats then fashionable was used for all Sterne's books, and may be presumed to express the novelist's own taste.

With the turn of the century the old system of printing and publishing disappeared, and authors with typographical ambitions were forced to plan their own book-production. In the first part of the period, Thomas Frognall Dibdin occupies an outstanding position, later the Pre-Raphaelite poets and painters expressed themselves typographically, and in minor degrees writers of leisure such as Edward FitzGerald and Frederick Locker-Lampson, without being typographers, showed sufficient interest in the design of their books to produce small personal variations of interest.

The number of 'typographically minded' authors in more recent years, though still small, is much greater and

[1] *Life and Times of Laurence Sterne*, Wilbur L. Cross (1924), i. 177.

more influential than in the first half of last century. It
includes John Ruskin, Robert Bridges, George Moore,
Bernard Shaw, Gordon Craig and, in addition to those
already referred to, artists and author-artists like Whistler,
Lucien Pissarro, Laurence Housman, Claud Lovat Fraser,
and, more recently, Eric Gill, all of whom, by insisting
upon their own taste and skill, have added something
valuable or interesting to the quality of common printing. It is not a very formidable list so far as numbers go,
but the interference of some of these authors and artists
has revolutionized typography. Without their influence
the modern typographer, or designer of books, who has
given a soul to mechanical printing, might not have
existed.

In all these instances there is evidence that the very
decided success attained was prompted by an understanding of the aims and limitations of the printer's craft.
The relationship between author and printer is intimate
and, whether a hand-set book or a machine-set book,
a hand-printed book or a power-printed book, will live
longest in the regard of book-folk, it is certain that the
desirable qualities of a book whose typography has
been inspired by the same genius which created the text
will always be valued. This, of course, does not mean
that such inspirers of 'straight' printing as Robert Bridges,
George Moore, and Bernard Shaw wish to be courted
for their typographical charms. When they were thinking typographically they were not thinking of printing
but of reading apropos of their own writing.

They were trying to discover what counterfeit presentment of their ideas or imaginings would put them in the most memorable and convenient relation with their readers. 'The *page* is in service to what is printed on it', says Walter de la Mare, 'and therefore to the eye of the reader'; and it should 'contain just so much printed matter as will preclude any active attention being distracted to its margins.' Whether the writers named thought it out in those terms or whether they acted instinctively for the best, the object was the same. They wanted their books to have a character of their own and to be typographically readable. They achieved their object when they remained artists without becoming artistic, and when they blended patterns of types with designs of materials, without dependence upon extraneous ornament or opulent accessories: when, in fact, they acted upon Eric Gill's advice and left Beauty to look after herself.

THOMAS FROGNALL DIBDIN

THOMAS FROGNALL DIBDIN THOUGHT TYPOGRAPHICALLY IN the grand manner. He favoured large paper, believed William Bulmer's edition of *Milton*, in folio, to be 'the most beautifully executed volume of the British press',[1] and frankly confessed his pride 'in the maintenance of a particular reputation for beautiful works'. He quotes with approval Sir Richard Colt Hoare's description of the first *Bibliographical Tour* as 'quite a Gentleman's Book',[2] which indeed it was; he is agreeably amused when an unfriendly reviewer calls him 'the Beau Brummel of living authors, in regard to the glossy splendour' of his publications,[3] and he reflects with obvious enjoyment on the exclusive character of the publications of the *Société des bibliophiles français*, the French version of the Roxburghe Club, whose members 'unite vigorously in keeping them from the touch of vulgar hands'.[4] Yet, if we may believe him, his laudable desire was not so much to produce fine books as to 'awaken the love of the literature of past days' and 'to set wealthy and well-educated men a-stirring to collect materials' which might otherwise 'moulder in oblivion'.[5] His volumes of 'beauty, singularity, and perfection of workmanship'[6] were thus decoys. He gilded the scholastic pill with the best materials of book-production, aided and abetted by that great printer William Bulmer, who did some of his finest work for him.

1 *Reminiscences* (1836), i. 348. 2 Ib. ii. 679. 3 Ib. ii. 688.
4 Ib. i. 480. 5 Ib. i. 285. 6 Ib. i. 274.

The editions of his principal works were issued by subscription on large and small paper, the Large Paper copies being 'embellished' with extra plates and sometimes with what he calls 'most effulgent workings in red'.[1] This sort of effulgence developed early, and he boasted that he was 'the first of living authors, who in the year 1810, in the first volume of the *Typographical Antiquities*—resumed, or restored', that 'good old diversity of colour in our printed volumes'.[2] His love of printing is nowhere so clearly revealed as in this liking for 'workings in red'. The examples in the *Bibliographical Decameron* (1817) are particularly effective, 'not only exquisite,' he says, 'but most difficult, execution; and it were doubtful at the time whether there was another press in Europe which could match them'.[3] The expense of those workings was 'equal to that of working the entire *sixteen pages* of text; because the whole forme must be shifted, and a distinct *operation*, however minute, ensues.' In an estimate for printing, William Bulmer, knowing his customer, gives warning that 'in the above calculation, there is no reservation made either for alterations—printing in red, blue or yellow—or indeed any extra or fanciful propensity which a gentleman of fertility of genius may be pleased to indulge in, by way of bothering the poor printer'.

There is no doubt that Dibdin chose good printers for the same reason that he chose good paper-makers and

---

1 The issue price of the *Bibliographical Decameron* was £12 12s.; of the *Aedes Aethorpianae*, £6 6s. small and £12 12s. large paper; and of the *Tour in Normandy &c.*, and the *Tour in England &c.*, £9 9s. small and £16 16s. large paper, and £3 13s. 6d. small and £7 7s. large paper, respectively.
2 *Reminiscences* (1836), ii. 603.   3 Ib. i. 490.

good binders, because he knew good from bad, as was perhaps inevitable in a bibliographer whose pleasure and business it had been for many years to examine and describe the typographical masterpieces of all ages. But examination and description of the treasures in Lord Spencer's collection were not the whole of an association with great books. Dibdin had a romantic affection for books, and he lived so passionately among masterpieces of typography at Althorp that they became part of his consciousness, so that he would 'dream of the printing presses at Mentz, Hamberg, Rome and Venice'[1] and wake up fancying himself Fust or Pfister.[2] And when he edits anonymously the *Judgment and Mercy for Afflicted Souls* of Francis Quarles, he does so under the name of Reginald Wolfe, a King's printer in the reign of Edward VI.[3] This enthusiasm for printing was shared by his friend and patron, Earl Spencer, who looked upon himself as a 'typographical antiquarian' rather than a reader and a scholar.

With such an experience at such a time it is surprising and gratifying to find that Dibdin resisted all temptations to lapse into archaisms or ornamentation. However much his style in typography depended for effect upon size, and the area of his books was invariably justified by their illustrations and general purpose, the printing was always simple and direct. If he loved splendour of format he loved a scholarly completeness and accuracy as well; but he loved both more when beautifully printed. He was conscious always of an act of homage towards great

1 *Reminiscences* (1836), i. 494.   2 Ib. i. 508.   3 Ib. i. 258. Dibdin wrongly attributes Wolfe to the reign of Henry VIII.

books, and collectors looked upon his seven-volume work on the Althorp Library[1] as the monument it is. 'Two things will ever continue to console me', he says in his *Reminiscences*, 'in some of the results which followed the publication of the *Aedes*.[2] I had exerted myself to the utmost to execute with fidelity and ability the task assigned to me. I had, in turn, erected a *Monument* to the name of Spencer . . .

> . . . quod nec Jovis ira, nec ignes,
> Nec poterit ferrum, nec edax abolere vetustas'

But this love of good printing, although developed by familiarity with fine specimens of the past, was inborn, for he expressed interest in the typography of his earliest, as well as his latest, works. As a young man, he tells us, he 'loved . . . to dwell upon beautiful, large paper, and vellum copies' and 'could have undertaken a journey to Mecca to see a first Homer, or a first Plato, printed upon vellum'; and the first edition of his first book, the *Introduction to the Classics* (1804), was 'beautifully printed in a tabular form'.[3] He went into raptures over the large-paper copies of the second edition, his first 'essay of the kind' which 'giving an air of splendour to the book, seemed to render it worthy, in the estimation of its author, of being dedicated to a Nobleman of great literary and senatorial distinction'. The nobleman was

1 This famous library was bought in 1892 by Mrs. John Rylands for £250,000 and is now preserved in the Rylands Library in Manchester as a memorial to her husband.   2 *Aedes Althorpianae*, 3 vols. (1822–3), sequel to *Bibliotheca Spenceriana; or a Descriptive Catalogue of the Books Printed in the Fifteenth Century, and of many valuable First Editions, in the Library of George John Earl Spencer, K.G., &c., &c., &c.*, 4 vols. (1814–15.)   3 *Reminiscences* (1836), i. 206.

Earl Spencer, who 'declined the intended honour'. Dibdin's enthusiasm was not reduced by this rebuff. 'I cannot now remember what were my *gains*', he writes, 'but I *can* remember that, when the first copy of it, upon large paper (bound by Herring, in morocco, with gilt leaves), was brought to me, I thought all my toil abundantly remunerated by the very appearance of the volume', and he compares his 'heart-swelling delight' to that of Cardinal Ximenes when he received the first perfect copy of his *Polyglot Bible*.[1] Even when a book of his appears through the ordinary trade channels he keeps an eye upon the typography and he rejoices in the preface to his second work, a translation of Fénelon's treatise *De l'éducation des filles* (1805), that 'it is accompanied by considerable beauty of type and paper, and elegance of ornament'.[2]

Dibdin's *typophilia* is at its best in his tributes to William Bulmer, printer of his principal bibliographical works, whom he called the English Jensen. After referring to the engravers, the 'ingenious artists (Mary, Ebenezer, and John Byfield) who have so effectually contributed to the splendour' of the *Bibliotheca Spenceriana* (1814), he acknowledges his indebtedness 'still more to the celebrated Printer in whose Office it has been executed. Those who are able to appreciate the care and skill requisite to render volumes of this nature beautiful and accurate, will readily admit that the present are executed in a manner worthy of the high reputation of the Shakespeare Press.'[3]

1 *Reminiscences* (1836), i. 209–10. 2 Ib. i. 217. 3 *Bibliotheca Spenceriana* (1814), Preface, vii–ix.

In his *Reminiscences* Dibdin once more praises the *Bibliotheca Spenceriana*. 'I will frankly—and perhaps foolishly as well as fondly—avow', he says, 'that I had never before seen a book which so entirely possessed and delighted me from its typographical and graphical beauties of every description. It was also a grand octavo volume in point of size; being of an imperial form—and the paper was as good as the printing. . . . Gay has observed

> Where yet was ever found a Mother
> Who'd give her booby for another?

It may be so: in fact it *is* so!'[1] But when the first volume of the *Bibliographical De-cameron* (1817) was published he is equally enthusiastic, concluding the preface with a further and well-earned tribute to Bulmer: 'For *one* feature which the Work possesses, he may boldly challenge the criticism, and bespeak the approbation, of the skilful: the *typographical execution* of it has been rarely equalled, and perhaps never surpassed.'

Such enthusiasm may

THE
BIBLIOGRAPHICAL
DECAMERON;
OR,
Ten Days Pleasant Discourse
UPON
ILLUMINATED MANUSCRIPTS,
AND
SUBJECTS CONNECTED WITH
EARLY ENGRAVING, TYPOGRAPHY,
AND BIBLIOGRAPHY.

BY THE
REV T. F. DIBDIN.

VOL. I.

LONDON:
PRINTED FOR THE AUTHOR, BY W. BULMER AND CO.
Shakspeare Press:
AND SOLD BY G. AND W. NICOL, PAYNE AND FOSS, EVANS, JOHN AND
ARTHUR ARCH, TRIPHOOK, AND J. MAJOR.
1817

Title-page of *Bibliographical Decameron*, first edition, large paper. 10″×6″.

1 *Reminiscences* (1836), ii. 573.

seem excessive to some modern readers, but it must be remembered that gusto was then permitted and writers, professional as well as amateur, thought italics and capitals necessary for purposes of emphasis. If he used exaggerated language he did not necessarily exaggerate, and he was not alone, for all his friends and subscribers, in letters which he rightly calls 'effusions', use similar terms. Dibdin was but the leader of a chorus.[1] So when he says that the fourth volume of the *Typographical Antiquities* 'came out with no lack of original splendour, and the copies on *large paper* towered as high, and luxuriated as proudly, as their predecessors', he is doing little more than emphasize facts. Such opulent language can be used legitimately to describe his major publications. Dibdin was an enthusiast. He enjoyed the pomp and circumstance of book-production and did not make a secret of it. If his own circumstances and the method of publication by subscription forced him to use some of the tricks of the high-powered salesman, the design of his books is not allowed to suffer. He never 'traded down' and, although he sometimes aimed so high as to risk pomposity, he is entirely free from the later vice of preciosity.

Dibdin often, too often, wrote about book-collecting so gushingly that even in his own day, when that sort of thing was tolerated, he laid himself open to the charge of dealing in flapdoodle, but his sentiment for printing

---

1 'If the Gods could read, they would never be without a copy of the (*Bibliographical*) Decameron in their *side pocket*!' George Henry Freeling to Dibdin. *Reminiscences* (1836), ii. 650.

was neither sentimental nor entirely mercenary. He was as willing to take part in the drudgery of the printing-office as he was to undertake the labours of research, selection of prints and their layout, in addition to the writing of his vast works; and although he obtained high prices for the volumes, whether on small or large paper, his lavish expenditure on paper, engravings, and author's corrections showed a disregard for profits which was far from 'businesslike' and from the point of view of economics would have been more appropriate to a pluto-crat than to a parson. Despite many textual lapses and errors of fact, he was a tireless corrector of proofs and took an active part in the design of the pages; at all times he was in consultation with his printers. The *Biblio-graphical Decameron* aroused all sorts of difficulties in the 'mechanical arrangement of the press, so as to make *just room* for the "thousand and one" wood blocks with which it seemed to be studded. What cuttings out, or cuttings in—now compression—now enlargement—in all and every way.

Double, double, toil and trouble.'

At these conferences Bulmer would be present with his foreman and proof-reader, Thomas Turner, and his chief compositor, Smith, and the charges for author's correc-tions, that ancient irritant in the association of author and printer, were for once incontestable. Dibdin was not, however, solely interested in the printing of his publications, he was a book-designer in the modern sense, taking control of every operation from printing to selling. And as he chose the best printers, binders, paper-makers, and engravers, so when publishers are allowed to distribute his books, he chooses William Pickering and John Major, the most individual publishers

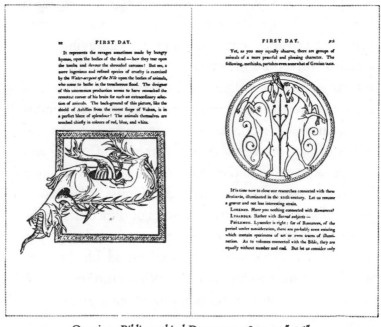

Opening, *Bibliographical Decameron*, 1817. 10″×6″.

of the day. His prospectuses are excellent alike in copy and typography, and in each of them he emphasizes the quality of the work advertised from the point of view of production. The announcement of the *Bibliographical Decameron* says that

'The Work has been at the Shakespeare Press for the last ten months, and is executed in a manner which has never been exceeded by any publication from the same distinguished quarter. The Artists engaged upon the Plates, whether upon Copper or Wood, will be found to have shewn themselves worthy of the reputation they have long enjoyed; and upwards of £2000 *already* expended upon these embellishments may give some idea of their number and excellence.'

And it is a further sign of his interest in all the parts of his books that he did not set to work on the book 'in right earnest' or issue a prospectus 'announcing its probable appearance', until he had 'bespoke some *one hundred and twenty reams* of that beautiful paper upon which the reader sees it printed'.[1] He had an equal interest in type-faces, and this extract from the announcement of his *Bibliotheca Spenceriana* has quite a modern note: 'It will be printed with a new type in the Elzevir-form, and in the best manner of the Shakespeare Press, upon paper manufactured purposely for it.'[2] The volumes are issued in boards but there are always a number specially bound by Lewis or Herring, who, like Bulmer among printers, are in the front rank of their craft. He is so proud of the *Bibliographical Decameron*, 'the paper, the workmanship at the press and with the copperplate printer, the variety, in form, colour and character, of the ornaments', when he sees them first 'united in one solid body', that he is anxious for the work to reach subscribers 'in as beautiful a condition as possible'. He therefore prevails 'upon them to have their copies bound by Charles Lewis, in the first instance, as being the safest passport to their own hands'.[3] And when one of his books, the first edition of *The Library Companion*, for instance, does not come up to standard, he does not hesitate to say so. That particular

---

1 *Reminiscences* (1836), ii. 598-9.   2 Ib. i. 492.   3 Ib. ii. 619-20.

THE BIBLIOMANIA;

OR,

𝕭ook=𝕸adness;

CONTAINING SOME ACCOUNT OF THE

HISTORY, SYMPTOMS, AND CURE OF

THIS FATAL DISEASE.

In an Epistle addressed to

RICHARD HEBER, Esq.

BY THE

REV. THOMAS FROGNALL DIBDIN, F.S.A.

Styll am I besy bokes assemblynge,
For to have plenty it is a plesaunt thynge
In my conceyt, and to have them ay in honde:
But what they mene do I nat understonde.
Pynson's Ship of Fools. Edit. 1509.

LONDON:

PRINTED FOR LONGMAN, HURST, REES, AND ORME,
PATERNOSTER-ROW,
BY W. SAVAGE, BEDFORD BURY, COVENT-GARDEN.
1809.

Price Four Shillings, in Boards.

Title-page of *The Bibliomania*, first edition. $8\frac{7}{8}'' \times 5\frac{5}{8}''$.

BIBLIOMANIA;

OR

𝕭𝕺𝕺𝕶 𝕸𝕒𝕕𝕟𝕖𝕤𝕤:

A BIBLIOGRAPHICAL ROMANCE,

IN SIX PARTS.

Illustrated with Cuts.

___

BY THE REV.

THOMAS FROGNALL DIBDIN.

INTERIOR OF THE BODLEIAN LIBRARY
I pity all our great ones and rich men that know not this happiness HEINSIUS

LONDON: PRINTED FOR THE AUTHOR,
By J. M'Creery, Blackhorse-court, Fleet-street;
AND SOLD BY MESSRS. LONGMAN, HURST, REES, ORME,
AND BROWN, PATERNOSTER-ROW.

___

1811.

Reproduced from the large paper edition of *Bibliomania*, 1811. $10\frac{1}{2}'' \times 7''$.

work was 'unadorned with cuts and unattractive from beauty of paper or printing'.[1]   But, on the whole, he is well satisfied with his efforts and in spite of his love of a fine-looking book he never forgets that the main object of a book is to be read. 'It is from a conviction of the good, theoretical and practical, which these pages contain, that the author of them now appears, in a garb not unworthy, I trust, of his reputation, to attract the notice, and to secure the respect of the virtuous reader.'[2] He hopes the 'embellishments' of the *Typographical Antiquities* 'will be found to keep pace with its intrinsic worth'.[3]

During the first quarter of the nineteenth century Dibdin's sumptuous volumes were eagerly bought and treasured by a race of patrician scholars and bookmen whose kind is now almost extinct, yet his scholarship and the intrinsic value of his works were often questioned by his contemporaries. Alexander Dyce called him 'an ignorant pretender, without the learning of a schoolboy, who published a quantity of books swarming with errors of every description', and a French critic remarked that the *Bibliographical Tour* 'would have been a capital book if there had been no letterpress'. Such opinions are still repeated, especially by those who have never taken the trouble to read him, and to some extent they are true. He was not a scientific bibliographer and the conditions under which his books were produced did not make for precision. On the other hand, we must go to Dibdin if we would form an idea of the character and extent of

1 *Reminiscences* (1836), ii. 714. 2 Ib. ii. 831. He is referring to his edition of *Thomas à Kempis*, incidentally one of his typographical failures. 3 Ib. i. 286.

book-collecting at one of its notable periods, and for that reason alone his works can never be wholly ignored. Despite the flamboyancy of his prose, the best of his books, such as the *Bibliomania*, the *Bibliographical Decameron*, and the *Tour in France and Germany*, must always interest the reader who is a collector or interested in the phenomena of collecting, and, if he is a typophil as well, he will rejoice in the beauty of their design and printing. And if Dibdin loses his place as a pioneer of bibliography, he will more than hold his own as a designer of books and an inspirer of good printing.

III

EDWARD FITZGERALD

EDWARD FITZGERALD PUBLISHED SEVERAL BOOKS AND pamphlets for his own amusement and at his own expense, and passages in his letters suggest that he was as fastidious a critic of printing as of poetry or music. His early books carried the imprint of Pickering, in itself a commendable choice. Further evidence of his personal rule over the typography of his own works is finally, if negatively, shown in the absence of all individuality in the editions of *Omar Khayyám* which appeared immediately after his death. His best-known book, the subject, as we shall see, of so many disputes with his publisher, was to become a victim of typographical extravagance and vulgarity. A convenient size and the accident of popularity so exposed FitzGerald's *Omar* to the enterprise of publishers who saw profit in pretty, artistic, decorated, or illustrated editions, that a collection of them, since the first issue went out of copyright, would form a complete exhibition of every typographical vice of the last fifty years.

Edward FitzGerald had no formal theory of printing, but scattered references in his letters show that he had definite ideas concerning the form and appearance of a book and that he took a keen interest in the details of production.[1] Criticism of his publisher is hedged about with

---

1 In giving instructions to Bernard Quaritch about the binding of *Salaman* with 'the new *Omar*' (1872) he stipulates: 'If *half bound* the back may be lettered (lengthways you know).' *Letters from Edward FitzGerald to Bernard Quaritch*, ed. C. Quaritch Wrentmore (1926), 22.

protestations of the insignificance of his works, but the diffidence with which he arrests suggestions of self-appreciation must not be taken too seriously. His coy-ness is often conceit in reverse gear. When, for instance, in acknowledging receipt of a copy of *Omar* (1872) from Bernard Quaritch, he adds, 'I can only say that I doubt you have put him into a finer Dress than he deserves—and that some other Critics will have their Bile raised to say so—if they take any notice now of the old Offender', and later when he describes the first American edition as 'Much Ado about very Little', it is safe to assume that he was far from displeased. At the same time, he has a very real objection to pretentiousness in the format of his own or other people's books.

His taste in printing was the opposite to that of Dibdin. He wants his books to be 'nicely printed and proportioned' and, above all, to 'come modestly forth'. Ostentation repelled him, and he was morbidly shy of self-advertisement. When he decided to let Quaritch publish a small edition of a translation of *Agamemnon* he confided to Fanny Kemble that 'the worst is, he *will* print it pretentiously, I fear, as if one thought it very precious'.[1] His fears increased when he saw the proofs, 'for, whatever the merit of it may be, it can't come near all this fine Paper, Margins, &c., which Quaritch *will* have as counting on only a few buyers, who will buy—in America almost wholly'.[2]

It was this nervous concern for the modest bearing of his books which made him a critic of printing. He

---

1 *Letters of Edward FitzGerald to Fanny Kemble* (1895), 98.   2 Ib. 112.

RUBÁIYÁT

OF

OMAR KHAYYÁM,

THE ASTRONOMER-POET OF PERSIA.

Translated into English Verse.

LONDON:
BERNARD QUARITCH,
CASTLE STREET, LEICESTER SQUARE.
1859.

Title-page of *Omar Khayyám*, first edition. Issued in brown wrappers. $8\frac{5}{16}'' \times 6\frac{1}{2}''$

RUBÁIYÁT

OF

OMAR KHAYYÁM,

THE ASTRONOMER-POET OF PERSIA.

Rendered into English Verse.

SECOND EDITION.

LONDON:
BERNARD QUARITCH,
PICCADILLY.
1868.

Cover of *Omar Khayyám*, second edition. Issued in drab wrappers. $7\frac{1}{8}'' \times 5\frac{5}{8}''$.

RUBÁIYÁT

OF

OMAR KHAYYÁM,

THE ASTRONOMER-POET OF PERSIA.

Rendered into English Verse.

THIRD EDITION.

LONDON:

BERNARD QUARITCH,

PICCADILLY.

1872.

Title-page of *Omar Khayyám*, third edition. 8⅜″ × 6¼″.

RUBÁIYÁT

OF

OMAR KHAYYÁM;

AND THE

SALÁMÁN AND ÁBSÁL

OF

JÁMÍ;

RENDERED INTO ENGLISH VERSE.

BERNARD QUARITCH; 15 PICCADILLY, LONDON.

1879.

Title-page of *Omar Khayyám*, fourth edition. 6⅞″×5″.

infused a few books with individuality, because he himself was individual and knew what he liked. The brown paper, humblest of materials, used to cover the first edition of his *Omar*, is the symbol of his coyness about that great work; it also expresses a firm conviction that all books should be unpretentious and keep their place. This fastidiousness comes out most clearly, as might be expected, in his letters to Quaritch, and especially in those dealing with the publication of the fourth edition of *Omar Khayyam* in 1879, the last to be issued during FitzGerald's lifetime.

He could never rid himself of the idea that he had allowed his publisher to have too much of his own way and that if he did not put his foot down the editions of the quatrains might grow inconveniently in size and magnificence. So without divesting himself of his protective diffidence he sets out to get his own way. He discusses size of page, rules and ornaments, advertisements, number of copies; and he requires that 'any Alterations' he makes 'be strictly done'. He is very particular about the colophon of the book—a red seal bearing the words 'The truth God only knows', and it is only after some trouble that he succeeds in getting the words enclosed in the plain circle of his own devising. And to show that he is prepared even to sacrifice a lifelong whim in favour of simplicity in the printed page, he proposes to abandon the capital letters he is so fond of using for nouns in his letters and poems, because 'it is contrary to the usage of far better men than myself, and looks ugly'.

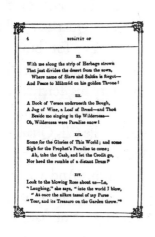

II.

With me along the strip of Herbage strown
That just divides the desert from the sown,
Where name of Slave and Sultán is forgot—
And Peace to Máhmúd on his golden Throne!

III.

A Book of Verses underneath the Bough,
A Jug of Wine, a Loaf of Bread—and Thou
Beside me singing in the Wilderness—
Oh, Wilderness were Paradise enow!

XII.

Some for the Glories of This World; and some
Sigh for the Prophet's Paradise to come;
Ah, take the Cash, and let the Credit go,
Nor heed the rumble of a distant Drum!

XIV.

Look to the blowing Rose about us—"Lo,
"Laughing," she says, "into the world I blow,
"At once the silken tassel of my Purse
"Tear, and its Treasure on the Garden throw."

XV.

And those who husbanded the Golden grain,
And those who flung it to the winds like Rain,
Alike to no such aureate Earth are turn'd
As, buried once, Men want dug up again.

XVI.

The Worldly Hope men set their Hearts upon
Turns Ashes—or it prospers; and anon,
Like Snow upon the Desert's dusty Face,
Lighting a little hour or two—was gone.

XVII.

Think, in this batter'd Caravanserai
Whose Portals are alternate Night and Day,
How Sultán after Sultán with his Pomp
Abode his destin'd Hour, and went his way.

XVIII.

They say the Lion and the Lizard keep
The Courts where Jamshyd gloried and drank deep;
And Bahrám, that great Hunter—the Wild Ass
Stamps o'er his Head, but cannot break his Sleep.

Opening of *Omar Khayyám*, third edition, 1872. 8⅝″ × 6¼″.

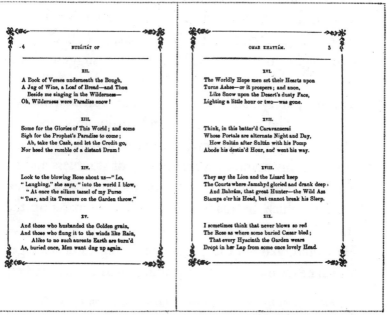

III.

A Book of Verses underneath the Bough,
A Jug of Wine, a Loaf of Bread—and Thou
Beside me singing in the Wilderness—
Oh, Wilderness were Paradise enow!

XIII.

Some for the Glories of This World; and some
Sigh for the Prophet's Paradise to come;
Ah, take the Cash, and let the Credit go,
Nor heed the rumble of a distant Drum!

XIV.

Look to the blowing Rose about us—"Lo,
"Laughing," she says, "into the world I blow,
"At once the silken tassel of my Purse
"Tear, and its Treasure on the Garden throw."

XV.

And those who husbanded the Golden grain,
And those who flung it to the winds like Rain,
Alike to no such aureate Earth are turn'd
As, buried once, Men want dug up again.

XVI.

The Worldly Hope men set their Hearts upon
Turns Ashes—or it prospers; and anon,
Like Snow upon the Desert's dusty Face,
Lighting a little hour or two—was gone.

XVII.

Think, in this batter'd Caravanserai
Whose Portals are alternate Night and Day,
How Sultán after Sultán with his Pomp
Abode his destin'd Hour, and went his way.

XVIII.

They say the Lion and the Lizard keep
The Courts where Jamshyd gloried and drank deep:
And Bahrám, that great Hunter—the Wild Ass
Stamps o'er his Head, but cannot break his Sleep.

XIX.

I sometimes think that never blows so red
The Rose as where some buried Cæsar bled;
That every Hyacinth the Garden wears
Dropt in her Lap from some once lovely Head.

Opening of *Omar Khayyám*, fourth edition, 1879. 6⅞″ × 5″.

His dislike of 'all big Books' was the cause of the numerous but amiable squabbles with Quaritch, who favoured quarto sizes, as we have seen, for business reasons. FitzGerald is precise on the problem of size, and although he continues to make modesty his defence, the preference is finally a matter of convenience, smaller books being more readable. 'All *Verse*', he tells Quaritch, 'should be in a *handy*, pocketable size: as much better Verse than mine is generally printed in. And I have a dislike to see my minor things swelled out into 4to margin as if they were precious things. You said in a former letter that I could choose my own shape of Book: and, unless you care to trouble yourself with further Argument on so small a matter, I am for the usual size.'[1] He is trying to enforce his own taste for the design of a new edition of *Omar* which was to include for the first time the translation of Jami's *Salámán and Ábsál*. 'The two might go into a smaller shape', he suggests, 'than *Omar* has yet been in.' He wanted the size 'now generally used for poetry', and with no more ornament within or without. The new edition (1879) finally appeared in a smaller quarto cut somewhat to resemble octavo. Few books, in his opinion, were worthy of stoutness and he enforced slimming upon the volumes in his own small library, which he made smaller still by separating the sheep from the goats after a manner entirely his own. He would take out the pages containing those passages which he thought worth re-reading, bind them together,

1 *Letters from Edward FitzGerald to Bernard Quaritch*, ed. C. Quaritch Wrentmore (1926), 59.

and throw the rest away! The process was admirably adapted to the limitations of space in the little cabin of his sailing-boat *Scandal*, in which he spent many happy hours between Lowestoft and the Crouch.

There is no attempt here to put Edward FitzGerald on

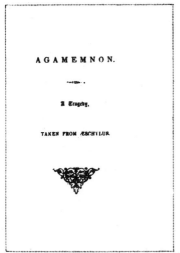

AGAMEMNON.

A Tragedy,

TAKEN FROM ÆSCHYLUS.

POLONIUS:

A COLLECTION

OF

WISE SAWS AND MODERN INSTANCES

LONDON
WILLIAM PICKERING.
1852

Title-page of *Agamemnon*, first edition. $7\frac{1}{4}'' \times 4\frac{7}{8}''$.	Title-page of *Polonius*, first edition. $6\frac{7}{8}'' \times 4\frac{7}{8}''$.

a pedestal as a typographer. He contributed nothing of importance to printing, and what he did was incidental to his needs as a reader and his whims as a writer. But, little as he did, he is a good example of an author who tried to steer printer and publisher between the shoals of shoddy and pretentiousness at a time when there was little taste in printing. The result was not always happy, for in trying to avoid one evil he sometimes slipped into the other. For instance, his fear of ostentation is shown in the uninviting form chosen for his edition of the

Readings in Crabbe. But, at their best, his editions of *Polonius* and *Omar Khayyám* have that sort of charm and clarity which must always please the reader of books, and possibly the not too fastidious typographer as well.

IV

JOHN RUSKIN

RUSKIN WAS THE INSPIRER OF THE CRAFTSMANSHIP OF
William Morris and thus, indirectly, started the typographical movement as it manifested itself in the private
presses of the eighteen-nineties. He was interested in
printing for its own sake from childhood. At a tender age
he liked the look of print and laboriously copied type
for his own pleasure 'as other children draw dogs and
horses'. His attitude towards typography was the same
as that which he adopted for all kinds of work, and if
we are to judge by what he says we shall be forced to
conclude that he was more concerned about the ethics
than the aesthetics of printing. He was also, as I have
mentioned already,[1] something of a typophobe and
classed the invention of printing with the invention of
gunpowder as one of the prime causes of many of the
evils of a civilization which, in his opinion, was none too
good. 'The abominable art of printing' was a bother from
its inception for, by releasing and universalizing what
he called the 'gabble of fools' as well as by encouraging
uniformity, it gave our bewildered world an apparently
irresistible opportunity of taking the wrong turning.
Ruskin, however, did not propose that we should
abolish printing; he strove by example and precept to
make it a gracious, intelligent, but not too accessible
medium for the inculcation of moral precepts, the expression of imagination, and the interpretation of ideas. To

1 See p. 43, *supra*.

M

clear the way for that good work he protested against the 'plague of cheap literature', and was convinced that 'we ought not to get our books too cheaply'. 'No book', he said, 'is ever worth half so much to its reader as one that has been coveted for a year at a bookstall, and bought out of saved half-pence; and perhaps a day or two's fasting.'[1] It is not surprising, therefore, that for the greater part of his life, though he made some exceptions, he was opposed to the publication of cheap editions of his own works.

Aesthetically, he did not practise what he preached, or we should never have known the convenience of the Ruskinian typography as it was produced for him by his friend and publisher George Allen at Orpington, or the quiet dignity of the olive-green cloth of the standard editions, or the pleasant grey pamphlet papers which bear his name. The style of his typography, like that of his later writings, is obviously the product of a taste which was passionately moved by notions of good behaviour. He believed that taste was not only a part and an index of morality, but that it was the only morality.[2] Ruskin was a puritan with a sensitive social consciousness. Taste and quality in production were for him virtues to be practised like truthfulness and honesty, and his typography is the well-behaved expression of that opinion.

The printing which came under his control escaped the influence of those ideas of Gothic decoration which had such an ill effect upon the work of architects who

1 *Political Economy of Art* (1857), 87.   2 *The Crown of Wild Olive* (1866), ii. 74.

were moved by his doctrines. But his books had, at one time, a narrow escape, for he flirted with the idea of decorated types and pages. 'It seems to me', he told Alfred Tuer of the Leadenhall Press, 'that a lovely field of design is open in the treatment of decorative type— not in the mere big initials, in which one cannot find the letters, but in delicate and variable fantastic ornamentation of capitals, and filling of black spaces or musically-divided periods of sentences and breadths of margins.' If Ruskin had followed that trail we might have had an extension of the quaintness and archaism already favoured by Tuer instead of a simplicity of design which, no matter what fashions intervene, will always command respect.

Ruskin believed that design 'is human invention, consulting human capacity', and he expressed the idea very clearly in the design of his books. But, notwithstanding his interest in printing and the care he is known to have taken over the production of his books, he wrote very little on the subject. Almost every kind of art and craft is cited and analysed in his works—painting, sculpture, building, weaving, gardening, reading, governing, fighting—but printing which was so near to him as a writer and reader is ignored. The omission is all the more curious when we remember that he used the symbol of a book, in *The Seven Lamps of Architecture*, to expound a method for the criticism of buildings, just as others have used architecture as the analogy of a book. 'The criticism of a building', he says, 'is to be conducted precisely on the same principles as that of a book.' It is true that he is thinking of the contents rather than of

PRÆTERITA.

OUTLINES OF
SCENES AND THOUGHTS

PERHAPS
WORTHY OF MEMORY
IN MY PAST LIFE.

BY

JOHN RUSKIN, LL.D.,

HONORARY STUDENT OF CHRIST CHURCH.
AND HONORARY FELLOW OF CORPUS CHRISTI COLLEGE, OXFORD.

VOLUME III.

CHAPTER IV
JOANNA'S CARE.

GEORGE ALLEN,
SUNNYSIDE, ORPINGTON, KENT.
1889.

Price One Shilling. ⌈28.

Cover of *Praeterita,* first edition. The parts were issued in grey wrappers. $9\frac{1}{2}'' \times 6''$.

the design, but even here there is evidence that contents and design are associated, for he advises critics to 'read the sculpture', but first to discover whether it is legible or not.[1]

It would not be difficult, however, to make precepts for printing out of many passages scattered about his works on other arts or crafts, and more particularly out of his theory of design. 'If you give one grain of weight too much, so as to increase fatigue without profit or bulk without value—that added grain is hurtful.' That is the problem behind his idea of human invention consulting human capacity, and it is the quintessence of book designing as the masters and as Ruskin himself practised it. For principles which may be applied to printing equally with any other craft you may open his essays or letters anywhere. Thus: 'Whatever the material you choose to work with, your art is base if it does not bring out the distinctive qualities of that material.' 'A thing is worth precisely what

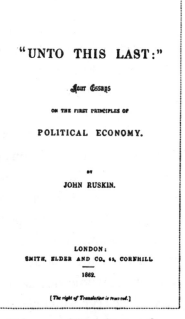

"UNTO THIS LAST:"

Four Essays

ON THE FIRST PRINCIPLES OF

POLITICAL ECONOMY.

BY

JOHN RUSKIN.

LONDON:
SMITH, ELDER AND CO., 15, CORNHILL
1862.

[*The right of Translation is reserved.*]

Title-page of *Unto this Last*, first edition. $6\frac{5}{8}'' \times 4\frac{1}{8}''$.

1 See Notes, p. 272, *infra*.

it can do for you; not what you choose to pay for it. 'The real good of all work,[1] and of all commerce, depends on the final intrinsic worth of the thing you make, or get by it.' 'The proof of a thing's being right is . . . that it excites us, wins us, or helps us.' 'The true forms of conventional ornament are, that they consist in the bestowal of as much beauty on the object as shall be consistent with its Material, its Place, and its Office.'

When Ruskin allowed himself to be guided by these principles the results were admirable, but where he departs from them and allows himself to imitate rather than be inspired by the past the results, as in the binding of the *Seven Lamps of Architecture*, are deplorable. His binding was usually plain and wholesome, and where he ventured upon a little decoration, as in the first edition of *Unto this Last*, he produces a pleasing effect. The stamped gilt frames of both front and back covers, though derived from hand tooling, which theoretically he should have objected to, enclose the book pleasantly and comfortably, and complete that 'harmony of proportion' which he demanded in architecture. Some of his books, such as *Fors Clavigera* and *Praeterita*, were issued in parts, but he always used plain buff paper with little or no ornamentation. Occasionally, he lapsed into large paper for reasons which have never been explained,[2] but his typography was, on the whole, normal and straightforward. He rarely used a fancy type, his lines were always adequately leaded, and he invariably gave the reader his first consideration.

1 See Notes, p. 274, *infra*.   2 It is not improbable that Ruskin had an eye on the collector.

126 IV. JOANNA'S CARE.

and loving nature secured in her relations with all those around her; and in the habits of childish play, or education, then common in the rural towns of South Scotland: of which, let me say at once that there was greater refinement in them, and more honourable pride, than probably, at that time, in any other district of Europe;* a certain pathetic melody and power of tradition consecrating nearly every scene with some past light, either of heroism or religion.

* The following couple of pages, from 'Redgauntlet,' put in very few words the points of difference between them and the fatally progressive follies and vanities of Edinburgh:—

"'Come away, Mr. Fairford; the Edinburgh time is later than ours,' said the Provost.

"'And come away, young gentlemen,' said the Laird; 'I remember your father weel, at the Cross, thirty years ago. I reckon you are as late in Edinburgh as at London; four o'clock hours, eh?'

"'Not quite so degenerate,' replied Fairford;

IV. JOANNA'S CARE. 127

And so it chanced, providentially, that at this moment, when my mother's thoughts dwelt constantly on the past, there should be this child near us,—still truly a child, in her powers of innocent pleasure, but already so accustomed to sorrow, that there

'but certainly many Edinburgh people are so ill-advised as to postpone their dinner till three, that they may have full time to answer their London correspondents.'

"'London correspondents!' said Mr. Maxwell; 'and pray, what the devil have the people of Auld Reekie to do with London correspondents?'

"'The tradesmen must have their goods,' said Fairford.

"'Can they no' buy our own Scottish manufactures, and pick their customers' pockets in a more patriotic manner?'

"'Then the ladies must have fashions,' said Fairford.

"'Can they not busk the plaid over their heads, as their mothers did? A tartan screen, and once a year a new cockernony from Paris, should serve a countess; but ye have not many of them left, I think. Mareschal, Airley, Winton, Wemyss, Balmerino—ay, ay, the countesses and

Opening of *Unto this Last*, first edition. $6\frac{5}{8}'' \times 4\frac{1}{8}''$.

Cover of *Unto this Last*, first edition. Green cloth, gilt. $6\frac{5}{8}'' \times 4\frac{1}{8}''$.

V

WHISTLER

TO MOST PEOPLE WHISTLER IS A WIT WHO PAINTED PICTURES. They know him for his gibes at the critics, his sallies with Oscar Wilde, his responses in the courts of law, his marginalia in the memoirs of artists he disliked, and his letters to the press. If they remember his pictures at all it is the *Nocturne in Blue and Gold,* or more frequently the *Mother* or the *Carlyle.* But that is a narrow view of a genius who was one of the most versatile artists of his time and whose gifts went beyond pictures to express themselves in the decorative and other arts. Whistler was, in fact, an artist in all his being and doing. Some men are artists in relation to what they do as painters or poets and in all other respects they are indistinguishable from the rest of us. Whistler made an art of himself. Everything he did was art. Like Oscar Wilde, he was, in Arthur Symons's phrase, 'an artist in attitudes'. In dress he was a dandy, in manners a poseur; his conversation was designed in epigrams and irritants, and his letters were as mannered as his talk and his nocturnes. In the decoration of his home he leapt over the Pre-Raphaelites to the Functionalists of to-day and his writings, though a by-product, are conceived in a prose of extraordinary poise and clarity. When he projected his personality into pictures he became an acknowledged master of painting, etching, and lithography, and he was also a distinguished black-and-white illustrator at a time when that art was at its best.

He became a typographer to further the interests of the exhibitions of his own pictures, for which he designed invitation cards, posters, and catalogues. He invented a style of his own and applied it without much variation

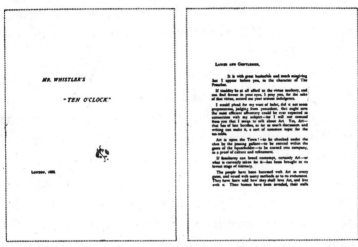

Title- and first page of *Mr. Whistler's Ten O'Clock*, first edition. $7\frac{5}{8}'' \times 5\frac{5}{8}''$.

to all his publications whether pamphlets or catalogues or books. The famous butterfly signature, which played such an important part in his typography, appeared first on the invitation card of his exhibition in 1874. The equally famous brown paper covers appear for the first time on the pamphlet, *Whistler* v. *Ruskin—Art and Art Critics* (1878).[1] But the characteristics of the format which ultimately became that of the *Ten O'Clock* (1888) were of later growth. They began to take shape with the publication of *Art and Art Critics*, in 1878; and from

---

1 Whistler was not the originator of brown paper wrappers. They were used by Edward FitzGerald in 1859 for the first edition of his *Omar Khayyám*. See p. 76, *supra*.

1881 onwards the format was adopted for all the exhibition catalogues. Whistler's typographical evolution ended triumphantly in the designs for *The Gentle Art of Making Enemies* (1890) and *The Baronet and the Butterfly* (1899),[1] a style which was followed by Pennell in the *Life of Whistler* as well as in his edition of *The Whistler Diary*.

His contacts with book-production were not accidental. They arose out of that continuous publicity campaign carried on by Whistler the business man in favour of Whistler the artist. He was one of the first artists to realize that it pays to advertise, and it was only natural that his advertisements should partake of his artistry. As we have seen, he designed the printed matter for his exhibitions as carefully as he designed the scheme for hanging his pictures, and he was further associated with printing as an illustrator, particularly of periodicals such as *Once a Week* and *Good Words*, and, in addition to the covers of his own works, he designed two for novels by Elizabeth Robins and another for Charles Whibley's *Book of Scoundrels*, all at the request of William Heinemann. But the genius for typographical design revealed in the exhibition catalogues might have ended with *Mr. Whistler's Ten O'Clock*, had it not been for the piracy of his letters to the press, of extracts from his responses in the *Ruskin v. Whistler* case, and of scraps of his conversation, by an American journalist residing in London

---

1 *The Gentle Art of Making Enemies* was printed at the Ballantyne Press, but *The Baronet and the Butterfly* was printed in Paris by Valentine, and published by Louis-Henry May, 11 Rue St Benoît.

named Sheridan Ford. It was the accident of that piracy which precipitated Whistler into the front rank of book-designers, for it was to secure his copyrights that he published *The Gentle Art of Making Enemies.*

When he came to design a format for his own writings he invented a style which, although obviously in the French convention, was as personal as his pictures, his mural decorations, or his prose. The Whistler attitude is maintained, yet his typography is objective to the extent of living up to the chief purpose of a book. On the other hand, the printing as well as the format seem to be inevitable for what he had to say and the way he said it, and, as Whistler's prose style is always that of a talker rather than a writer, so he manages to get into his typography a conversational lightness. An outstanding characteristic of this typography is an impression of decoration without the use of ornaments or illustrations except the signature Butterfly. Comparing Whistler's edition of *The Gentle Art of Making Enemies* with what Joseph Pennell calls Sheridan Ford's 'undistinguished' pirated edition,[1] Pennell says that the former contains on every page evidence of Whistler's care in carrying out his ideas of book decoration. Whistler must have brooded

1 *The Gentle Art of Making Enemies,* edited by Sheridan Ford (New York, Frederick Stokes & Brother, 1890). Fcp. 8vo. Grey wrappers. The typography of this rare book is not entirely 'undistinguished', for it includes the Butterfly, and in some other details it so much resembles the pattern, of the authentic edition, that it may be assumed Whistler either made suggestions for the design before the quarrel with his editor, or that he took a tip from him as he did in the title, which appeared first as a phrase in a letter from Ford to his first printers, Field & Tuer, one of whom, probably Alfred Tuer, suggested that it would make a more attractive title than that originally chosen by Ford: *The Correspondence of James McNeill Whistler.*

over his pages[1] until they became the individual and charming patterns they are. 'The trouble he took over his pamphlets and catalogues is almost unbelievable', says Pennell, 'and he gave no less to his letters—margins ample, the division into paragraphs symmetrical, punctuation effective, the Butterfly where it told.' And he again emphasizes Whistler's sense of decoration by saying that for him 'there could exist no form of art that was not decorative'. Whistler made patterns of print, but knowing that the object of print is to be read he produced his effects with the maximum of simplicity. It may have been that sort of simplicity which Oscar Wilde called the last refuge of complexity, but although mannered, as anything by Whistler must have been, it is an agreeable manner, simple and readable as well as beautiful, avoiding not only the challenging impudence which the artist deliberately adopted towards his fellows, but the artistic pitfalls of those times. Decoration was for him the harmonious arrangement of materials, not something added to them.

Whistler did something more than dodge artistic perils. Whilst Morris was depending on the past for the future of printing, Whistler created a style out of the present which has more of the spirit of good book-building than any other original product of that period of typographical liveliness. Max Beerbohm, who disclaims, I regret to say, the title of book-lover, and even brags about it, makes an exception in favour of *The Gentle Art of Making Enemies*.

1 See Notes, pp. 274–5, *infra*.

'Such a book I treat tenderly, as one would a flower. And such a book is, in its own brown-papered boards, whereon gleam little gilt italics and a little gilt butterfly, Whistler's *Gentle Art of Making Enemies*. It happens to be also a book which I have read again and again—a book that has often travelled with me. Yet its cover is as fresh as when first . . . it

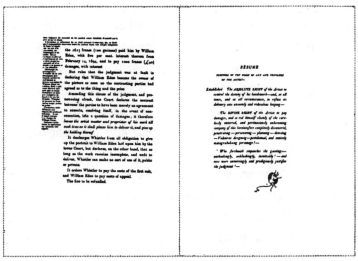

Opening of *The Baronet & the Butterfly*. 8″ × 6⅛″.

came into my possession. A flower freshly plucked, one would say—a brown-and-yellow flower, with a little gilt butterfly fluttering over it. And its inner petals, its delicately proportioned pages, are as white and undishevelled as though they never had been opened.'[1]

A. J. A. Symons makes this remarkable book the starting-point of his exhaustive study of 'The Typography of the Nineties', adding, however, the somewhat sweeping assertion that it was Whistler's 'personal example, more than any other, that influenced later comers' in typography.[2]

[1] *Yet Again*, 104–5;   [2] *Fleuron* (1930), vii. 87.

Whether that statement is exaggerated or not, Whistler's originality is incontestable, and, more important still, the originality of his design was achieved with the common materials and craftsmanship of commerce. Whistler did not demand hand-made paper, new typefaces, specially prepared ink, hand presses, or vellum from the Vatican, before creating a beautiful book. He took what was best for his purpose from the tradesmen and without ornamental trickery made an arrangement in types and papers and ink which is as beautiful in its way and as appropriate for its purpose as that *Arrangement in Black and Grey* which was the description he gave to the portrait of his mother.

The two volumes which give Whistler a niche among book-designers, *The Gentle Art of Making Enemies* and *The Baronet and the Butterfly*, are almost identical in format. The size is small quarto and the type-area and length of lines are agreeable to the eye, though the margins are excessive. This spacious *mise-en-page* with carefully posed signatory Butterfly and marginal notes is doubtless derived from his own letters. It is an appropriate derivation for a book which is so personal as to suggest indiscretion, as though one were permitted to peep into the author's private correspondence or overhear his personal remarks. It was deliberate of course: you were expected to peep and pry. That was part of the Whistler pose. Equally relevant, however, is the harmony achieved between printing, paper, and binding, and the binding is perhaps the most original and satisfying contribution made by him to the design of books. The materials, as I have said, are commonplace: brown paper and ordinary bookbinder's cloth of a dull yellow shade, but they are combined so proportionately as to produce a usable covering of subdued grace and charm. The yellow cloth just covers the spine, being gripped at the hinges by the brown paper of the boards. There is no imitation or suggestion of half- or quarter-leather binding. It is a treatment of cloth and paper without pretence. It is functional binding or casing, but it is not bleak or 'mechanistic'.

The evolution of the Butterfly signature is an impressive characteristic of Whistler's typography, and interesting because of its origin; for what began as a signature became a typographical device as well as an exclamatory comment. It was 'evolved', Pennell tells us, 'from the simple interweaving of the initials J. M. W.', and 'designed to explain the text to which it referred'. In its larval stage the Butterfly was no more than a signature, and it was some time before this famous insect took upon itself the witty characteristics of its creator, but, after the chrysalis is broken, the imago appears fully equipped with a sting in its tail for a career of criticism and commentation. It is not only made to point a moral and adorn a tale by juxtaposition, but each specimen is drawn specially for its commentatory purpose, as though the artist stood back at a sally, with his favourite exclamation, 'Amazing!' uttered with appropriate inflexion for the occasion, and as *cul-de-lampe* to the report of the *Ruskin* v. *Whistler* trial the Butterfly has alighted upon a farthing—the amount awarded to the plaintiff for

EDEN VERSUS WHISTLER

THE BARONET & THE BUTTERFLY

A VALENTINE WITH A VERDICT

PARIS

Cover of *The Baronet & the Butterfly*. Brown paper boards, yellow spine, gilt. 8″ × 6⅛

EDEN VERSUS WHISTLER

THE BARONET & THE BUTTERFLY

A VALENTINE WITH
A VERDICT

PARIS
LOUIS-HENRY MAY
11, rue St-Benoît

Title-page of *The Baronet & the Butterfly,* first edition. $8'' \times 6\frac{1}{8}''$.

damages. The genius of Whistler as a typographer is revealed at its happiest in the use of this exclamatory Butterfly. It is an example of decorative wit and plays two parts with equal success. The artist has adapted a convention of the etcher to the *mise-en-page* of a book. The Butterfly is used as etcher or engraver use the *remarque* on a proof. But Whistler had also given special significance to the placing of the signature on his pictures and considered it of such decorative value that he would discuss the exact position with his intimates as though a masterpiece depended for its success upon this final touch.

VI

ROBERT BRIDGES

ROBERT BRIDGES WAS INTERESTED IN PRINTING FOR THE greater part of his life and his contribution to typography is not only notable in itself but, like his interest in phonetics, it is definitely related to his work as a poet. He supervised the printing of all his works and designed the format of most of them, even when they were printed at the University Press, Oxford. But his interest in typography was not confined to his own works, nor to the publications of the Daniel Press, with which he was so closely associated; it was felt even by the University Press itself. The present Printer to the University brackets him with W. W. Greg and A. W. Pollard as one of 'the three men who have done most to encourage the taste and accuracy of Oxford Printing during the last twenty or thirty years'.[1] That influence has always been in the interest of the reader. His pages are beautiful examples of typographical design, and it is a tribute to the poet's genius for printing that they are an invitation to read rather than a display of typographical ingenuity.

For many years Robert Bridges was a friend and neighbour of that distinguished amateur of printing, C. H. O. Daniel, Provost of Worcester College, Oxford, and many of his poems made their first appearance with the imprint of the Daniel Press. But the imprint implied something more than the ordinary relationship of author and publisher. Poet and printer, if not partners, were

1 John Johnson, *Robert Bridges and the Oxford University Press* (1930).

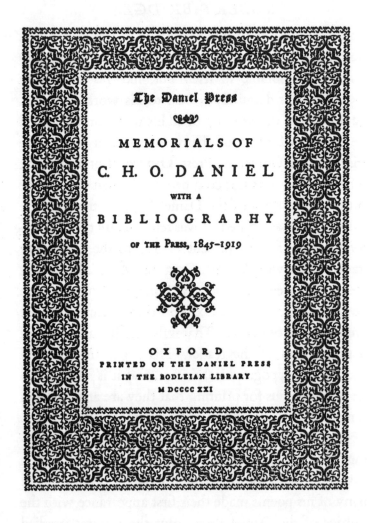

The Daniel Press

MEMORIALS OF

C. H. O. DANIEL

WITH A

BIBLIOGRAPHY

OF THE PRESS, 1845–1919

OXFORD
PRINTED ON THE DANIEL PRESS
IN THE BODLEIAN LIBRARY
M DCCCC XXI

Title-page of The Daniel Press *Memorials of C. H. O. Daniel.* $9\frac{1}{8}'' \times 7''$.

allies in a memorable typographical adventure. Bridges contributed to the famous *Garland of Rachel* in 1881, and his work is represented in fifteen of the fifty-eight major publications of the press during its maturity, beginning with *Prometheus the Firegiver* (1883) and ending with the

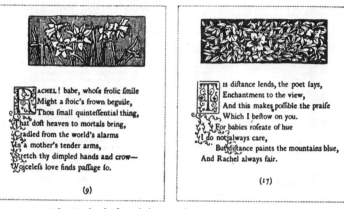

ACHEL! babe, whofe frolic fmile
Might a ftoic's frown beguile,
Thou fmall quinteffential thing,
That doft heaven to mortals bring,
Cradled from the world's alarms
In a mother's tender arms,
Stretch thy dimpled hands and crow—
Voiceless love finds paffage fo.

(9)

IS diftance lends, the poet fays,
Enchantment to the view,
And this makes poffible the praife
Which I beftow on you.
For babies rofeate of hue
I do not always care,
But diftance paints the mountains blue,
And Rachel always fair.

(17)

The Garland of Rachel, Daniel Press, 1881. $8\frac{3}{4}'' \times 5\frac{1}{2}''$.

Peace Ode Written on the Conclusion of the Three Years' War (1903). This average of nearly two volumes a year over the period covered represents by far the highest production of the press for one author; the next highest being the three volumes each of Canon Richard Watson Dixon and Sir Herbert Warren, and the two each of Francis William Bourdillon and Margaret L. Woods.

To what extent Robert Bridges influenced the Daniel Press is not revealed, so far as I am aware, in any written statement, but from internal evidence it would be safe to assume that his influence was considerable; it was also salutary because it made for simplicity of design by laying emphasis upon the text and how it should be read. Daniel, it should be recalled, was not a typographical reformer. His press was a hobby, and it was the personal character of his work which accidentally made him a pioneer of the revival of printing. Sir Herbert Warren observes that printing was 'his *parergon* and pastime', and also the means of 'the artistic expression of his leading gifts and

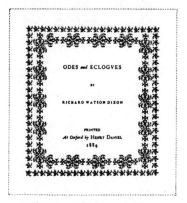

Title-page of *Odes and Eclogues*.
Reduced from 8½″ × 6¾″.

The Growth of Love, Daniel Press, 1890, showing Robert Bridges's use of black-letter. Reduced from 8⅝″ × 6¾″.

his whole nature'.[1] It was none the less a hobby, and none the worse, even if we have to admit that some of the books reveal the preciosity and self-consciousness of typographical toy-books. This is said to define, not to decry. The least of the Daniel books have their place, if only on the bric-à-brac shelf.

The Daniel Press books associated with Robert Bridges have, in the main, upheld the traditions of good printing without departing from the established characteristics of the press. The probability is that Bridges found in the

1 *The Daniel Press: 1845–1919* (1921), 7.

press an instrument which he thought might be used to express his own ideas of printing, and in Daniel himself a willing supporter. There is good evidence for the inference, and as he is known to have liked a well-arranged page, and to have taken a keen interest in the technique of printing, it is not surprising that new characteristics in the typography of the Daniel Press coincided with the publication of books by Bridges. There was above all a change from the amateurish and haphazard to the professional and workmanlike. Pages were better balanced, 'signatures' were adopted, and an ordered simplicity took the place of naïvety.

The move towards simplicity is noted by Falconer Madan in his comment on the *Poems* (1884), a work which was published between the *Odes and Eclogues* of Richard Watson Dixon and the *Poems* of Henry John Patmore, both issued in the same year. Madan writes: 'The almost entire absence of ornaments prevents this edition—which is of special interest as being the author's own anthology —from appearing as attractive as the two preceding. As the two prospectuses (nos. 112, 113) state, it is uniform with the *Prometheus* (no. 7), which is equally unadorned, no doubt in each case by the author's desire.'[1] The assumption that this 'unadorned' printing was actually 'by the author's desire' is proved by subsequent events. Bridges was no more a printing reformer or revivalist than Daniel. His interest was that of an author who wished to be read in the right way, and in one instance, at least, it is possible that he used a type-face to correct the *tempo*

1 Ib., 96.

for the reading of his own poems, as later he used specially designed types to express his own theories of phonetics,[1] without adding to the comfort of the reader.

Robert Bridges adhered to the practice of letting a simple yet gracious and friendly typographical arrangement act as the medium between himself and his readers. In the main he continued his allegiance to the Fell types discovered neglected at the Clarendon Press, and restored to active service by Daniel in 1876. There was, however, one outstanding departure from this rule. It takes the form of the use of black-letter for the *Shorter Poems*, issued in five parts (1893–4), and the *Hymns* (1899). In view of Bridges's preference for roman characters, this lapse into medievalism requires some explanation. The type-face used has distinction and the printing is fine in quality and design, but it is an unwarranted archaism impeding easy contact with the poet, and acceptable only in distant prospect, like the Houses of Parliament or St. Pancras Hotel. Madan's comment on the use of black-letter for the *Shorter Poems* explains without accounting for this departure. He describes the volume as one to be desired because 'the black-letter' gives 'just the check to hasty reading which thoughtful and elaborate poems need'. Knowing as we do that Robert Bridges had definite convictions on the printing of verse, there can be no harm in supposing that his use of black-letter was purposeful and based upon the desire to check hasty reading as suggested by Madan, but it is an alarming doctrine, and fortunately one which is not likely to be

1 See Notes, pp. 275–6, *infra*.

accepted for general application or pushed to its logical conclusion; otherwise a large body of our poetry would be read only by a limited hierarchy of cloistral students, who might ultimately be forced into the ironical position of having to issue the results of their black-letter reading of, say, *Sordello* and the *Book of Ahania* in roman, if they wished them to be read by others. Trial by black-letter will never do. It is the business of the reader, not the printer, to administer that 'check to hasty reading which thoughtful and elaborate poems need'; any further discipline which may be necessary should be inherent in the poem, not externally applied.[1]

The publication of the *Shorter Poems* was a large job for so small a press; but it was obviously thought out and conducted with care, and there can be little doubt that the choice of type had the approval of the author. Black-letter was not unknown to the press; it appears in many title-pages, often with tolerable decorative effect; and Robert Bridges seems to show interest in it elsewhere. There is a curious instance in the title-page of *An Address to the Swindon Branch of the Workers' Educational Association* (1916), which is set in upper and lower case roman and italic, with the exception of the name of the association. This name inexplicably bursts into gothic as if the W.E.A. had suddenly gone monastic! The pamphlet

[1] The idea of a speed limit for poetry is widely held, and Francis Meynell, believing that 'poetry should not . . . be easily read' (*The Nonesuch Century*, 51), printed the *Love Poems of John Donne* in Fell italics, 'not merely because those Fell letters are particularly pretty and characteristic, but because it has been thought right to entice, by their unusual form, a particular attention to the poetry, so that the sight should not lazily run along the lines with a lazy mind'. From the *First List of Nonesuch Books* (1923).

itself is a piece of correct Clarendon Press work of the period and calls for no further remark. Two years later Robert Bridges's address, given to the Tredegar and District Co-operative Society, on *The Necessity of Poetry* was also printed at the Clarendon Press, and here we have a piece of printing faultless in every way—simplicity and distinction without fortuitous aid; a perfect pamphlet. The title-page is set in Fell and the text in Scotch roman; sectional cross-heads are in roman and sub-sectional in italic.

Once good printing is practised, character and variety are matters of personal taste. Bridges's books, despite lapses into black-letter, are always typographically sound : for that reason it is possible to discuss them, sometimes with disapproval. *The Yattendon Hymnal* (1899) is an example. It is a quarto, printed at the University Press, Oxford, revealing thought, taste, and imagination in detail and as a complete work. Any criticism of such a book must seem ungrateful, if not mere cavil; but I feel that the beauty of

THE NECESSITY
OF POETRY
An Address given to the
Tredegar & District Co-operative Society
Nov. 22, 1917.
by
ROBERT BRIDGES
Poet Laureate

Oxford
At the Clarendon Press
1918

The Necessity of Poetry, a pamphlet designed as well as written by Robert Bridges. 7⅝″×4⅞″.

the music types of Peter Walpergen (which Bridges revived) and the roman of the Fell fount would have been sufficient to achieve the kind of dignity he obviously wished to give to the collection of old hymns. Relief from undue austerity could have been obtained by the use of a printer's flower, or other unobtrusive ornament. Simple beauty, in some instances unadorned, has been achieved on many pages, and those pages give a peculiar satisfaction not to be got from the more efflorescent. The separation of columns of verse by means of a line of flowers serves no purpose. It is fussy rather than decorative. Curiously and fortunately the book possesses pages of both settings, so that comparison is possible, and few will deny that those with the fewest flowers are the best. On the other hand, the pages with no flowers are perhaps a little bleak. In the more successful pages the flower functions as a tail-piece.

Bridges, however, has few such lapses. His pages are austere and quiet. Their beauty is in their proportions, and that beauty remains unimpaired even during his experiments with new types in the *Testament of Beauty*, and in the *Collected Papers*, which, unscrutinized, look as though they were printed in Russian characters. And he had not only convictions of his own, but he was ready to associate his work with that of the best typographers of his time, as, for instance, when he invited Emery Walker to design the title-pages and the lettering on the bindings of *The Spirit of Man* and the *Chilswell Book of Poetry*.

It is neither easy nor necessary to select any book for

special praise where the majority are so admirable, but perhaps the most satisfying of all the books which come under the typographical influence of Robert Bridges, rising as it does above all ordinary criticism, is *The Poems of Digby Mackworth Dolben* (University Press, Oxford,

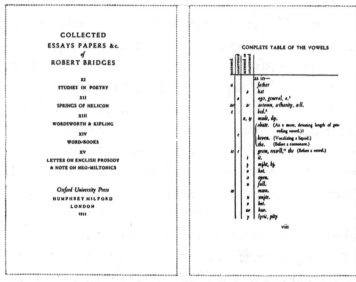

Title-page with contents, of Robert Bridges's *Selected Essays.* 7½″ × 5″.   Robert Bridges's Table of Vowels from *Selected Essays.* 7½″ × 5″.

1911). In this appropriate octavo, traffic between author and reader is made possible on the best terms. The bridge is gracious in form and convenient in structure—direct, simple, accessible. Here, if anywhere, Robert Bridges has achieved a satisfactory means of communication between writer and reader. If I were asked to give an example of a perfect marriage between printing and authorship, I should name this book.

VII

GEORGE MOORE

GEORGE MOORE GAVE CHARACTER TO THE TYPOGRAPHY OF
his later books by insisting upon definite ideas and principles of printing, and he has made the task of the commentator easier by recording his opinion of what good
printing should be. From the point of view of printing,
he is a brand from the burning recently salvaged. For
during the greater part of his life he made no effort to
give any sort of distinction to the printing of his books,
which began to appear in the typographically moribund
eighties. The printing of his novels and essays varies
from bad to passable, and when it is distinctive it is a
negative distinction. He must have heard much talk
about printing during his association with W. B. Yeats
and his circle in Dublin during the decade which followed
the Boer War; and familiarity with Elizabeth C. Yeats's
Dun Emer and Cuala Press publications, and the broadsides designed and decorated by Jack B. Yeats, may, and
indeed ought, to have encouraged him to think about
the design of books.

Moore's typographical awareness does not appear to
have been awakened until some time about 1915, and the
cause was not Irish printing but the graciously sophisti-
cated books of eighteenth-century England and France.
He soon, as might have been expected, developed ideas
of his own about type-areas and hand-setting.

The first-fruits are to be seen in *The Brook Kerith*
(1916), printed at the Riverside Press, Edinburgh, and

published in the year following. The founts and lay-
outs there adopted were used by him for the rest of his
life. He lacked invention and was not himself more
than an enthusiast for printing, yet his enthusiasm was
practical, and not above accepting help from others in
the production of editions of his own works. This is
evident in his willingness to allow some of his works to
appear in Nonesuch or Bruce Rogers formats. He took
an interest in the actual processes of printing[1] and expected the printers to be equally keen about the composition of his work, which he wrote and saw through
the press simultaneously. Francis Meynell records that
while *Ulick and Soracha* (1926) was at the printer's

'he came almost daily, hung up his square bowler hat and
settled down to read aloud to us the revisions he had made in
his last batch of proofs. Each time it was an entirely new text.
The first version was almost illiterate. The second grammatical
but undistinguished. The third a transfiguration. It was fas-
cinating to see the process of his composition at close quarters:
and our feelings were undisturbed by anxieties about the
printer's bill, for he had proposed at the outset that he should
pay for his own corrections. They exceeded the original cost
of the setting.'

There is nothing very original, or indeed very beautiful, about the design of Moore's own limited editions.
The chief characteristic is an elongated type-area, with
dubiously proportioned page-spacing, the upper and
lower margins being equal and the inner margins slightly
too wide. There is much to be said for a tall and slim
page when not too tall or slim. Tall slim pages have

---

1 See Notes, pp. 276-7, *infra*.

Title-page of *The Brook Kerith*, first edition. $8\frac{7}{8}'' \times 5\frac{11}{16}''$.

Title-page of *A Story-Teller's Holiday*, first edition. $8\frac{7}{8}'' \times 5\frac{1}{4}''$.

Title-page of *Ulick and Soracha*, Nonesuch edition. $5\frac{4}{5}'' \times 9\frac{3}{10}''$.

First page of *Ulick and Soracha*, ornament in red. $5\frac{4}{5}'' \times 9\frac{3}{10}''$.

more grace and are more readable than short fat ones. But nothing can be said for a disproportionate type-area, the laws here, with a narrow margin for idiosyncrasy to disport itself, being less ambiguous than in some other departments of typography. The defect was repaired by Moore in the second book of his typographical awakening, *A Story-Teller's Holiday* (Riverside Press, 1918), though even here the lay-out lacks balance. The elongation of type-area is obtained by the use of leads, and the lines are at least one em too narrow. The use of leads and lavish spacing between words gives the pages a light and under-inked effect which is aesthetically unpleasant and not easy to read. In appearance these pages recall those of a pamphlet run off the standing type of one of the sixpenny weekly reviews without the careful adjustment needed for the adaptation of long columns to a different size of paper.

The reason for George Moore's departure from ordinary or publisher's typography was, on his own admission, a sudden conversion to the printing methods of the eighteenth century as revealed in a book with a slim and graceful type-area which accidentally came into his hands. He liked the book so well that he used it as his model. But he also, and apparently at the same time, became a convert to hand-composing, believing henceforward that hand-setting (and presumably hand-printing, though he does not say so) produced more beautiful books than the mechanical processes.

'All the crafts are past and gone,' he says, 'even as the birds of Paradise that were slain for the decoration of cruel women,

GEORGE MOORE

Peronnik
the Fool

1　9　2　6

Title-page of *Peronnik the Fool*, designed by Bruce Rogers, in red and black. 9″× 5¾″.

so why waste further words upon them; but the craft of printing has not yet passed away, though sorely threatened by
machines endowed with so many late improvements that the

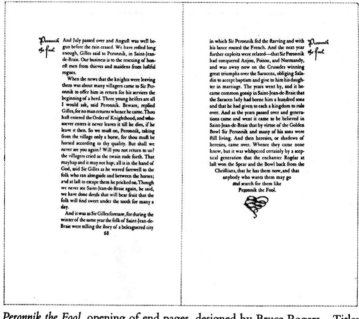

Peronnik the Fool, opening of end pages, designed by Bruce Rogers.   Titles
and device in red. $9'' \times 5\frac{3}{4}''$.

difference between machine-setting and hand-setting is not
easily recognisable by the uneducated.'[1]

And in reply to those who charge him with having given
his case away, since the difference sometimes even
deceives the experts, he has three replies.   One, that 'a
book is a knick-knack as well as a book', and therefore
should have the charm of a work of art; two, that a
'hand-set book is better to read', and a long book set by

[1] 'A Communication to Book Collectors', by George Moore, *Times
Literary Supplement*, March 10, 1921.

the machine is only bearable on a first reading; we cannot take it up a second time, for we miss that sense of delight that only the humanizing touch of a printer's fingers can give to a page, the faint irregularities which are the ultimate perfection; and three, that hand-set books will increase in value from the collector's point of view.

Obsessed with the idea of bric-à-brac, he is a convinced upholder of the fine arts, but his taste for fine printing is an afterthought. 'There are different kinds and sorts of books', he says, 'and although machine-setting is admirably suited to current literature it is, in my opinion, unsuited to the expensive book, which should be classed with Chelsea china, Battersea enamel, ormolu clocks, inlaid and painted furniture; the book that is, in a word, a knick-knack as well as a book.' And later on in this tardy excursion into typography Moore plays up to the collector, an unusual proceeding for an established author. 'I do not appeal to the philan-thropist but to the collector', he says; 'to him who invests his money in books that will be sold twenty years hence for three times the money that was paid for them; and I do well in appealing to the selfish interests, for they alone are valid; the best way to help others always being by helping yourself.'

These assumptions are as dubious as they are character-istic of a writer of genius who had the courage of his own opinions even when they might be ridiculous. He could be preposterous, but he was rarely inconsistent, and for that reason his most fantastic assumptions possess at least a relative verity. They have the virtue of being George

Memoirs
of My Dead Life

OF

*Galanteries , Meditations
and Remembrances
Soliloquies or Advice to Lovers,
~ with many miscellaneous Reflections
on Virtue & Merit*

BY

George Moore of Moore Hall C. Mayo

LONDON
Published by Heinemann.

Title-page of *Memoirs of My Dead Life*, first edition. 9″ × 5⅝″.

A Communication to
MY FRIENDS

I

On the occasion of an author publishing the uniform edition of his works, or a selection made by himself of the dozen, or better still, the half-dozen volumes that he looks upon as representing his art, it is usual, nay almost a politeness, for him to take his readers into his confidence and tell them how it came to pass that he retired from the ordinary amusements of life to writing about life.

I have often been asked if it was accident that turned me towards literature, or if it was an instinct within me that I could not control. The next questioner would ask if my characters are wholly imaginary, or copies of people I have met in my way through life. A third questioner would like to hear if I had encountered difficulties, and if so, how I had overcome them, arriving at last at success. All these questions provided me with the substance of a book about myself, but to write about myself I must look down the years through the spy-glass of memory for the day and the hour when I began to be myself.

First page of *A Communication to My Friends*, Nonesuch edition. $5\frac{3}{5}''\times9\frac{3}{10}''$.

PURE POETRY

an anthology edited by

George Moore

1924

The Nonesuch Press

30 Gerrard Street Soho W

Title-page of *Pure Poetry*, Nonesuch edition. $5\frac{3}{5}'' \times 9\frac{4}{5}''$.

Moore. They may be half-truths, but because they are firmly held and frankly stated they are more alive than many of their entire but otherwise emasculated brethren. To attack them is like hitting butterflies or thistle-down. They are recorded here as the opinions of a great writer upon an allied craft which writers of genius or otherwise too often take for granted. Holding fine theories about printing does not mean, however, an equal capacity to inspire good printing; if it did so, George Moore's printing might be as distinguished as his writing; but, interesting as it is, it is far from that. At the same time these tall volumes of his are not lacking in a sort of portly, almost pompous, elegance, but typographically they are not friendly. Ostentatiously hand-made paper and an unbending format tend to keep the reader at a distance. They are uncomfortable books, rather snobbish and, perhaps, a little meretricious. George Moore's reference to increasing value from the collector's point of view, and the method of the signed and limited edition adopted by him, almost convict him of profiteering.[1] But his quest of a beautiful format was not fruitless, for towards the end of his life Francis Meynell and Bruce Rogers, in the designs for *Ulick and Soracha* and *Peronnik the Fool*, gave him the typography of his dreams.

1 See Notes, pp. 277–8, *infra.*

VIII
BERNARD SHAW

BERNARD SHAW THROWS BACK TO WILLIAM MORRIS, TO THE
pre-Kelmscott-Caslon-Old-Face-Morris. It is generally
known among those interested in such things that he
controls his own books from their conception to their
incarnation in print. He buys his own printing and
binding, and the publishers receive the complete book,
market it, and account to the author for the proceeds.
The cycle of Shaw's egocentricity is thus complete
for, although he bases his ideas of printing on those
of Morris, they have been so transmuted that his
typography is as Shavian as his prose or his wit.
He has expressed his views on printing more than
once, and those views are implicit in the typographical
convention which he has adopted and carried out
with an integrity characteristic of the man and his
works.

During the greater part of his career Bernard Shaw has
been a believer in the solid black unleaded page, and for
forty years he has had his books printed by R. & R. Clark
of Edinburgh. He has held, with Morris and Emery
Walker, that good composition has the quality of good
masonry, and that the widest margin should be at the
bottom of the page, the narrowest at the back, the top
slightly wider, and still wider at the fore-edge though
narrower than the tail margin. All this is in the Arts
and Crafts convention. These rules were followed by
Morris when he co-operated with the Chiswick Press in

the printing of his prose romance, *The Roots of the Mountains* (1892).[1]

The principles which govern Shaw's typography were stated in an article 'On Modern Composition' contributed to the *Caxton Magazine* in 1902. 'The difference

Plays: Pleasant and Unpleasant. By Bernard Shaw. The First Volume, containing the three Unpleasant Plays.

London: Grant Richards, 9 Henrietta St. Covent Garden, W.C. 1898.

Title-page of *Plays Pleasant and Unpleasant*, first edition. 7″×4¾″.

Press Cuttings: a Topical Sketch compiled from the editorial and correspondence columns of the Daily Papers by Bernard Shaw, as performed by the Civic and Dramatic Guild at the Royal Court Theatre, London, on the 9th July 1909.

Archibald Constable & Co. Ltd. London: 1909.

Title-page of *Press Cuttings*, first edition. 6¾″×4⅝″.

between a well-printed page and an ill-printed one', he says, 'lies in the evenness of the block of colour presented by the letterpress.' He is emphatic in his dislike of what he calls 'that abomination of desolation, a rule'. He insists that 'the only thing that never looks right is a rule', and that 'there is not in existence a page with a rule on it that cannot be instantly and obviously improved by taking the rule out.[2] Even dashes, cherished as they are

1 See pp. 177 and 182, *infra*. 2 This objection has since been modified, for a 'swelled rule' is used in the titles of the Collected Edition of *Bernard Shaw's Works*.

by authors who cannot punctuate, spoil a page. They are generally ignorant substitutes for colons.'[1] These principles were first fully put into practice in *Plays Pleasant and Unpleasant* (1898) which was set in 10-point Caslon solid, and he adhered to them, with only slight variations such as the placing of headlines and pagination at the top of the page instead of in the margin and at the bottom respectively, for thirty years. But Bernard Shaw has not limited his taste to the printing of his books, he has controlled their design as well, and for thirty years also the Shavian octavos in their drab covers, at first of ribbed and then of plain cloth, have proclaimed themselves among brighter clad volumes much as low-toned clothes gave Napoleon prominence amid the more brilliant uniforms of the members of his staff.[2]

Like Morris, he pushes his theories to their logical conclusion. Shaw's early typography achieved distinction solely from the arrangement of types; there was no attempt at ornamentation, no flowers, no devices, no rules (of course), and only occasional illustrations. *Plays Pleasant and Unpleasant*, vol. i, has a photograph of the author in photogravure; *Three Plays for Puritans* (1901) has three photogravures; and in the separate edition of *Mrs. Warren's Profession* (1902) there are half-tone repro-

---

1 See Notes, p. 278, *infra.*   2 Whilst this uniform was maintained for the plays, occasional essays appeared in different binding. The original edition of *The Perfect Wagnerite* (1898) has an excellent cover in two shades of linen, fawn for the boards and blue for the spine; *Cashel Byron's Profession* (1901) is in red cloth; *The Commonsense of Municipal Trading* (1904) is in blue cloth, and *The Sanity of Art* (1908) in brown paper boards with cream cloth spine. All of the above, except *Cashel Byron*, eventually appeared in the first uniform edition.

ductions of photographs of the original cast. For the rest, type was allowed to speak for itself, or rather for G. B. S., with only one deviation. That deviation is in the terminal four advertisement pages of 'Works by the Same Author', which defy the usual conventions of such

Opening, *Plays Pleasant and Unpleasant.* $7'' \times 4\frac{3}{4}''$.

announcements by appearing vertically instead of horizontally. This may be symbolical, or just another example of Shavian anti-climax, in terms of print; but, on the other hand, it may be an advertising stunt.

Shaw achieves his desired but unnecessary degree of blackness in the copious prefaces and appendixes. The starkness of these pages is a tax upon the attention of his readers, who must have been grateful when, with the publication of *John Bull's Other Island* (1907), he introduced a generous sprinkling of cross-headings,

WHEN we come to the objections to equal division of income we find that most of them come to no more than this: that we are not accustomed to it, and have taken unequal division between classes so much for granted that we have never thought any other state of things possible, not to mention that the teachers and preachers appointed for us by the rich governing class have carefully hammered into us from our childhood that it is wicked and foolish to question the right of some people to be much better off than others.

Still, there are other objections. So many of them have been already disposed of in our examination of the schemes for unequal distribution that we need deal now with two only.

The first is that unless a woman were allowed to get more money than another she would have no incentive to work harder.

One answer to this is that nobody wants her to work harder than another at the national task. On the contrary, it is desirable that the burden of work, without which there could be no income to divide, should be shared equally by the workers. If those who are never happy unless they are working insist on putting in extra work to please themselves, they must not pretend that this is a painful sacrifice for which they should be paid; and, anyhow, they can always work off their superfluous energy on their hobbies.

On the other hand, there are people who grudge every moment they have to spend in working. That is no excuse for letting them off their share. Anyone who does less than her share of work, and yet takes her full share of the wealth produced by work, is a thief, and should be dealt with as any other sort of thief is dealt with.

But Weary Willie may say that he hates work, and is quite willing to take less, and be poor and dirty and ragged or even naked for the sake of getting off with less work. But that, as we have seen, cannot be allowed: voluntary poverty is just as mischievous socially as involuntary poverty: decent nations must insist on their citizens leading decent lives, doing their full share of the nation's work, and taking their full share of its income. When Weary Willie has done his bit he can be as lazy as he likes. He

72

will have plenty of leisure to lie on his back and listen to the birds, or watch his more impetuous neighbors working furiously at their hobbies, which may be sport, exploration, literature, the arts, the sciences, or any of the activities which we pursue for their own sakes when our material needs are satisfied. But poverty and social irresponsibility will be forbidden luxuries. Poor Willie will have to submit, not to compulsory poverty as at present, but to the compulsory well-being which he dreads still more.

However, there are mechanical difficulties in the way of freedom to work more or less than others in general national production. Such work is not nowadays separate individual work: it is organized associated work, carried on in great factories and offices in which work begins and ends at fixed hours. Our clothes, for instance, are mostly washed in steam laundries in which all the operations which used to be performed by one woman with her own tub, mangle, and ironing board are divided among groups of women using machinery and buildings which none of them could use single-handed even if she could afford to buy them, assisted by men operating a steam power plant. If some of these women or men were to offer to come an hour earlier or stay two hours later for extra wages the reply would be that such an arrangement was impossible, as they could do nothing without the co-operation of the rest. The machinery would not work for them unless the engine was going. It is a case of all or nobody.

In short, associated work and factory work: that is to say, the sort of work that makes it possible for our great modern civilized populations to exist, would be impossible if every worker could begin when she liked and leave off when she liked. In many factories the pace is set for the lazy and energetic alike by the engine. The railway service would not be of much use if the engine driver and the guard were to stop the train to look at a football match when they felt inclined that way. Casual people are useless in modern industry; and the other sort: those who want to work longer and harder than the rest, find that they cannot do it except in comparatively solitary occupations. Even in domestic service, where the difference between the unpunctual slacker and sloven and the model servant is very perceptible, the routine of the household keeps everybody up to a certain mark below which

73

Opening, *The Intelligent Woman's Guide*, first edition. 9″×6″.

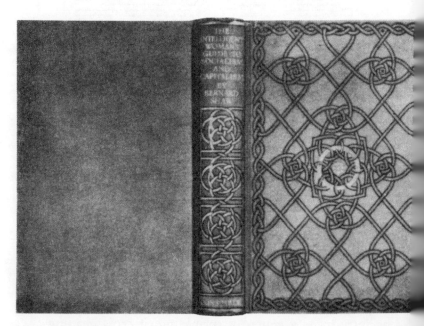

Cover of *The Intelligent Woman's Guide*. Sage green cloth, arabesque in emerald a[nd] gold, 9″ × 6″.

a device he has since continued to employ. The setting of the plays is admirable. The use of small capitals for the dramatis personae and italics within square brackets for stage directions give variety and convenience to the page.

With the publication of *The Intelligent Woman's Guide to Socialism and Capitalism*, in 1928, Bernard Shaw departs in several details from his favourite design, and there are greater changes to come. *The Intelligent Woman's Guide* is a medium octavo (9 × 6); plain boards have been abandoned and their place taken by a 'celtic' arabesque in green and gold. The familiar 10-point Caslon Old Face Solid has been supplanted by the much more readable 12-point solid. In these volumes the chapters open with four-line capitals projecting slightly into the margin according to the nature of the letter. It is a bolder and handsomer book than any of its predecessors, and the break with the past would seem to confess a desire on the part of the author for new typographical expression, and the austerity of unrelieved Caslon, drab covers, and squat volumes is abandoned. Their place has since been taken by a Standard Edition in royal 8vo, bound in red cloth, and set in Fournier 11 point on 12. Concessions to illustration and decoration are made in the folio *édition de luxe* of *St. Joan* with Charles Ricketts's designs for the stage settings in full colour, and *The Adventures of the Black Girl in her Search for God*, with decorations engraved on wood by John Farleigh. The type is the same as that used in the Standard Edition. Finally, there is a 'limited' *édition de luxe* of the complete

THE ADVENTURES OF THE BLACK GIRL IN HER SEARCH FOR GOD

THE ADVENTURES OF THE BLACK GIRL IN HER SEARCH FOR GOD

THE ADVENTURES OF THE BLACK GIRL
IN HER SEARCH FOR GOD

BERNARD SHAW

Cover of *The Adventures of the Black Girl*. Black paper boards, printed in white.
Designed by John Farleigh. $8\frac{1}{16}'' \times 5\frac{5}{16}''$.

trol his Arabs without enticing and intimidating them by promises of a delightful life for the faithful, and threats of an eternity
of disgusting torment for the wicked, after their bodily death, and
also, after some honest protests, by accepting the supernatural
character thrust on him by the childish superstition of his
followers; so that he, too, now needs to be rediscovered in his
true nature before Islam can come back to earth as a living faith.

And now I think the adventures of the black girl as revealed to
me need no longer puzzle anyone. They could hardly have happened to a white girl steeped from her birth in the pseudo-Chris-
tianity of the Churches. I take it that the missionary lifted her
straight out of her native tribal fetichism into an unbiassed contemplation of the Bible with its series of gods marking stages in
the development of the conception of God from the monster
Bogey Man to the Father; then to the spirit without body, parts,
nor passions; and finally to the definition of that spirit in the
words God is Love. For the primitive two her knobkerry suffices;
but when she reaches the end she has to point out that Love is not
enough (like Edith Cavell making the same discovery about Pat-
riotism) and that it is wiser to take Voltaire's advice by cultivating
her garden and bringing up her piccaninnies than to spend her
life imagining that she can find a complete explanation of the uni-
verse by laying about her with a knobkerry.
 Still, the knobkerry has to be used as far as the way is clear.
Mere agnosticism leads nowhere. When the question of the exist-

74

ence of Noah's idol is raised or the point, vital to high civilization, whether our children shall continue to be brought up to
worship it and compound for their sins by sacrificing to it, or,
more cheaply, by sheltering themselves behind another's sacrifice to it, then whoever hesitates to bring down the knobkerry
with might and main is ludicrously unfit to have any part in the
government of a modern State. The importance of a message to
that effect at the present world crisis is probably at the bottom of
my curious and sudden inspiration to write this tale instead of
cumbering theatrical literature with another stage comedy.

AYOT ST LAWRENCE,
 9th October 1932.

End pages of *The Adventures of the Black Girl*. $8\frac{1}{16}'' \times 5\frac{5}{16}''$.

writings, in which he reverts to his favourite Caslon type, but in 12 point, and there are two quarto omnibus volumes, one of the *Plays*, in Scotch roman, and the other of the famous *Prefaces*, in Fournier. These two portly volumes show a further departure from the Shaw

TOO TRUE TO BE GOOD,
VILLAGE WOOING & ON
THE ROCKS. THREE PLAYS
BY BERNARD SHAW

LONDON
CONSTABLE AND COMPANY
LIMITED

THE INTELLIGENT WOMAN'S GUIDE
TO SOCIALISM AND CAPITALISM
BY BERNARD SHAW

CONSTABLE AND COMPANY LTD. LONDON
1928

Title-page of *Too True to be Good*, standard edition. $8'' \times 5\frac{1}{16}''$.

Title-page of *The Intelligent Woman's Guide*, first edition. $9'' \times 6''$.

tradition of the solid page, for they are set in double columns.

The Adventures of the Black Girl is the most luxuriant of all Bernard Shaw's books, and, although little more than a pamphlet, it is one of the most attractive examples of contemporary typography. John Farleigh's illustrations are a genuine commentary upon the text and this relationship is maintained in the masterly decorations of the cover, title-page, and end-papers. A companion pamphlet, so far as size goes, the *Political Madhouse in America and Nearer Home* (1933), is not so successful. The cover is admirably lettered in a sans-serif character by Farleigh, but the typography is curiously lacking in distinction for a Shaw book. The only novelty, and not a satisfactory one, is the use without adequate justification of script initials on the title-page and for the opening of the lecture.

There is rectitude, rather than originality or charm, about Shaw's early typography. You are made to feel that it has been thought out rather than felt. It would seem almost as if the author had deliberately avoided any typographical hint of his own brilliance. The only idiosyncrasies are the use of spaced letters instead of italics for emphasis,[1] and a predilection for asymmetrical title-pages. The triumph of the text pages is the maximum of freedom from those straggling lines which are the bane of the printed play. This evenness has been attained by an almost laborious attention to the balance of lines, calling almost for as much ingenuity in the printing as in the writing. Indeed, Bernard Shaw's respect for good printing and a neat page is so pronounced that he confesses to having rewritten a passage in proof when lines were 'so widely spaced as to make a gray band across the page'. George Moore has more recently shown a like respect for the printed page.[2] The willingness of two such

---

[1] Shaw only uses italics for stage directions except in the case of the personal pronoun *I* which is italicized among spaced letters. In the Standard Edition he abandons spaced letters for emphasis and deliberately introduces a 'wrong fount', words requiring emphasis being set in Baskerville.
[2] See Chap. vii, *supra*.

masters of English to adjust their prose to the needs of good printing is evidence of a practical interest in the line of communication between author and reader. It suggests the sort of co-operation between author and his printer which may rescue us from any tendency towards the undue standardization of books.[1]

[1] The publication, in the *London Mercury* (March, 1937) of Bernard Shaw's letters to John Farleigh, 'concerning the illustrations to the *Black Girl*', are further evidence of his practical interest in typography.

IX

EDWARD GORDON CRAIG

GORDON CRAIG'S TYPOGRAPHY IN SOME OF ITS DETAILS RE-
calls the Arts and Crafts Movement—an Arts and Crafts
Movement which has taken a holiday in Italy. Without
being a definite link, it comes between the printing revival of the nineties and that of our own day. As a typographer he is romantic, with a leaning towards quaintness
and luxuriousness. The influence of the nineties is seen
in his liking for ornaments, but in the brown paper
boards and the treatment of the spine of the *Art of the
Theatre* (1911) there is reminiscence of the simple dignity
which we associate with the Whistler format. The introduction of colour into the monogram stamped on the
centre of the front cover is a charming individual characteristic; colour, for which he has genuine 'typographical'
feeling, might, indeed ought, to have been extended to
the *mise-en-page* of several of his books. But in spite of
incidental resemblances to other typographies Craig has
a style of his own, especially when he is responsible for
a complete book.

His interest in typography began in youth, and whilst
still in his early twenties he produced his first magazine,
The Page (1898), with 'original Poems, Prose, Music,
Woodcuts, Posters, Portraits, Bookplates, and other curious things'. Like other artists who have taken an interest
in printing, he thinks of a book in its entirety—even to the
bookplate, which he regards as a part of its architecture.[1]

1 *Nothing or the Bookplate*, by Edward Gordon Craig (1925), 10.

The use of the word architecture in relation to books is a good sign, because it recognizes the integrity of their various parts. In his essay on bookplates there are further expressions and hints which show a proper attitude towards books. Gordon Craig is a reader as well as a writer and an artist. He believes that 'a book is one of the best things we can meet', and, therefore, that 'everything to do with books is a delight'.[1] In the volume called *Books and Theatres* (1925) there are several passages which announce the bookman. In one of them he refers to himself and the friend with whom he was travelling in Italy, as 'lovers of that other world, the world of books'.

'To us', he says, 'a book contained all sorts of delight, for it is no matter that our subject was the Theatre—every province in this world, every state, is something rare and strange. Every book-lover knows all about it, and as this one is for book-lovers I need not re-tell them what they know. I need merely say in the fewest words that we loved the contents of our books, the paper—bindings—character of type-setting—the shape—weight and build of the book, its significant date—its initial letters—silk markers—condition—and even creak of its hinges. In fact we were like every other book-lover—*pazzi di libri.*'

His prescription for the demeanour of a bookplate, which, by the way, would be more accurately described as part of a book's furniture than of its architecture, might easily stand as a code of typographical behaviour.

'A large, imposing, and elaborately worked-up book-plate is annoying,' he says, 'just as a talkative, intellectual, highly cultured footman would be a nuisance. Suppose, on ringing

1 *Ib.*

the bell to enquire whether some friend was in, we had the doors thrown open for us by a remarkable man who, with charming gestures bade us enter, bade us be seated, took a seat by us and began to utter a number of very witty or profound things which held us spellbound and quenched any desire in us to proceed further into the hall. . . . We wish only one thing from the footman who opens the door. We wish to know, is he in, the master, or is he out, will he see us, or no. And the finely trained footman is the quietest, the least noticeable, one who makes himself small; the perfect footman is a gem.'[1]

As I have so often implied in these pages, a book is a gem when neither printing nor binding insists upon itself to the disadvantage of the author or the embarrassment of the reader who wishes to meet the author.[2] This principle is invariably carried out by Gordon Craig, but he has shown an occasional tendency towards unruly sizes for his books, as well as for over-decoration with undue emphasis on luxurious materials. Sometimes, as in the larger works dealing with the art of the theatre, size has been determined by the designs for stage settings or other illustrations.

The evolution of his typography may be conveniently studied in the three magazines for which he was responsible: *The Page* (1898–1900), *The Mask* (1908–1929), and *The Marionnette* (1918–1919). *The Page* represents his archaic period. It is crude and naïvely pretentious because

1 *Nothing or the Bookplate*, 2.   2 Gordon Craig expresses the same idea when reviewing the Nonesuch edition of William Blake's *Poetry and Prose*, where he approves of typographical 'points' which elude the reader 'through sheer quietness'. 'As a matter of fact,' he says, 'you won't see them: you'll see merely a most ordinary book—but exquisite: as you touch it you at once become conscious of a sense of perfection.'

it aims at distinction with uncertain taste and insufficient experience of book designing at a time when typographical influences were not always reliable guides. *The Page* has the weaknesses of the 'artistic' typography of the period, but if the design is unequal to that of *The Pageant*, or even *The Dome*, it was original enough to attract praise and blame from the critics. A critic in *The Dome* called it 'an imitation of nothing else in heaven or earth, or even in the place where young launchers of journalistic novelties affect to be most at home'. *Black and White* classed it among 'the frail dragon-flies of the magazine world', containing 'strange prose, stranger verse, and stranger illustrations', whose existence was justified by Gordon Craig's woodcuts which 'out-beggared the Beggarstaff Brothers'; whilst the *Weekly Sun* thought it 'a silly little magazine, which repeats some of the features of the "precious" school of late years, but repeats them with so much of the ignorance of the amateur that we think it worthy of comment as marking the lowest depth to which this movement has reached, or can reach'. These extracts prove at least that *The Page* stood out from the herd of periodicals, and also that a critique of printing had not yet affected the average reviewer.

The Mask, a magazine of the art of the theatre, printed and published in Florence, began as a folio and ended more comfortably as a quarto; but, as though uncertain of his taste in sizes, he goes to the other extreme in his later magazine, *The Marionnette*, which looks like a toy in foolscap octavo, and the effect is emphasized by the

covers of brightly coloured shiny paper.[1] The type used
is commonplace and, although there is no very obvious
design in the text, the use of rules and cuts and the general
proportion of the pages are intelligent and agreeable.
The Mask was a more elaborate experiment. Here Craig
expressed something of the richness he would bring into
all the arts of life and craft. In the last chapter of his book
On the Art of the Theatre (1911) he says:

> 'In place of vulgar materials, such as prose, coarse wooden
> boards, canvas, paint, *papier mâché* and powder, I would like
> more precious materials to be employed: Poetry, or even that
> far more precious Silence—ebony and ivory—silver and gold—
> the precious woods of rare trees—exquisite silks unusually
> dyed—marble and alabaster—and fine brains.'

A love of luxury and magnificence is a characteristic
of all Craig's work, and it reveals itself in his typography,
where it is often associated with a more dangerous love
of quaintness. Each of his magazines is fortified by an
édition de luxe, with special binding, paper, 'prints signed
by the artist', and other temptations. But of all the
ingredients which go to the making of a book Gordon
Craig gloats most over the paper, for which no other
typographer of our time, with the exception of Francis
Meynell, has had such authentic taste. One *édition de luxe*
of *The Mask* (1909) was 'printed upon a yellow hand-
made deckle-edged paper identical in appearance and
texture with that made in the district of Fabriano in the
year 1315'.

But this particular affection was at its best in books

1 There was also an *édition de luxe* in gold paper wrappers.

A typical Craig cover. Brown paper boards, black cloth spine, gilt. Device in colour and black. $8\frac{1}{2}'' \times 6\frac{1}{8}''$.

Opening of quarto series of *The Mask*, 1913. $9'' \times 6\frac{1}{2}''$.

Vol. One N.º 1. MARCH 1 9 0 8

THE MASK

A MONTHLY JOURNAL OF THE
ART OF THE THEATRE

EUROPEAN AGENTS.

LONDON. D. J. RIDER 36 St Martin's Court. Charing Cross Road. W. C.

SOLE GERMAN AGENT - SCHUSTER & BUFLEB. Nollendorfstrasse 31. W. BERLIN.

AMSTERDAM. KIRBERGER & KESPER. 134 Rokin.

LUNG' ARNO ACCIAIUOLI. FLORENCE.

PRICE ONE SHILLING, NET: MONTHLY

Cover of *The Mask*, No. I, edited and produced in Florence by Gordon Craig. 13">

THE MASK

THE JOURNAL OF THE ART
OF THE THEATRE.
VOLUME ONE, NUMBER ONE
MARCH 1908.

AFTER THE PRACTISE THE THEORY

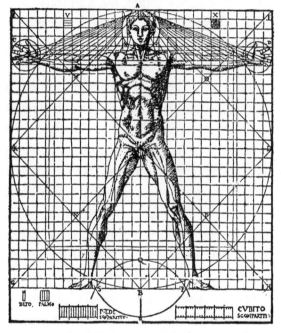

GEOMETRY. Beauty.... or Divine Demonstration, knows no confusion. It has the perfect balance. It remains true once and for ever.... needs no proof.... can reveal itself without words or arguments, and when we see l we again see Paradise. It is the dear Heaven. Science.... or Human Demonstration,t continually calling upon proof, trusting in many words, is as a restless Balance which continually rises and falls with the uncertainty of the centuries... the restless Terror; has become the only Evil.

First page of *The Mask*, No. I. 13"×9".

T

not destined for type, for Craig put all he knew about fine papers into that series of blank books which during the first decade of this century he issued from the Teatro Goldoni, Florence. These aristocratic note-books were 'intended for Artists who draw and Artists who write, being made from those fine Italian papers which, unobtainable in England, are found, even in Italy, only by experience and careful search'. Italy was explored for fine old or modern papers, and parcels, no matter how small, were bought up, and turned into blank books of various sizes bound in vellum or paper decorated in colour with floral or conventional designs printed by hand from the original wood blocks. Editions were limited to the quantity of paper obtainable, some being limited to from fourteen to forty copies. Sizes and prices varied according to purpose and cost. A catalogue was issued, probably the first of its kind, in which quantities and descriptions of the various volumes were given. This memorable enterprise, with its unstandardized pages made 'to turn and finger with delight' in sizes 'uncumbersome to the nicest hand' within covers 'bright and varied with colour and fresh design', has had no successful imitator.

Though the richness of *The Mask* is helped by paper of unusual distinction for a magazine, and by a generous use of illustrations, its individuality does not depend on a paper which is, perhaps, a little too impressive, or upon illustrations which are always well placed and organically related to the page, but upon an unusual and, in spite of quaintnesses, pleasing typographical design.

It is natural that the general appearance should be theatrical, but those who prefer a more restful page will not cavil when it is remembered that *The Mask* was a challenge rather than a contribution to periodical literature. Gordon Craig's books comport themselves less restlessly. They are devoted largely to the theatre, but histrionics are not included in their make-up.

Craig's influence on the design of those books and periodicals which came under his control is obvious, but you feel that the books suffer from arrested development. His influence with the publisher has not been strong enough to bring about a satisfying co-ordination of materials. It is as though he is either uncertain of what he wants to do, or certain, but prevented from doing it. Few of Craig's books live up to their covers, but when they do they are excellent. He is most original as a typographical designer in *The Mask*, where he has had fuller control over both the materials and the design of his publication.

X

ERIC GILL

ERIC GILL IS NOT CONTENT WITH BEING AN ARTIST. HE wants to know what he is about, and in his essays he seems to be reasoning as much with himself as with his reader. He is superlatively honest in the process despite a dialectical ingenuity which recalls that of a medieval schoolman, or John Ruskin. A reference to the panels of the Stations of the Cross which he carved for Westminster Cathedral as 'furniture, not decorations', is indicative of his attitude towards the arts. The remark appears in a defence of the architecture of the cathedral, or of as much of it as he can tolerate. Bentley, it seems, dreamed of a brick building encrusted with marble and carved ornaments, and where he went his own decorative way he was commonplace or even ridiculous. 'The outside of the building is almost entirely ruined by this absurd pandering to the appetite for ornamentation.' Gill likes the exterior 'as a piece of brick and concrete work' just as well as 'the great interior' before its pure architecture was smothered in coloured marbles and mosaics.

His career as well as his attitude towards the arts and crafts recall William Morris, but not always in the same way or for the same reasons. Like Morris, he began life in an architect's office, and, in addition to his distinguished achievement in sculpture (one of the few arts Morris did not practise), he is a letterer, a writer, a social reformer, and a typographer. But here the resemblance ends. Gill is never Gothic, least of all when designing letters or types. 'Lettering is for us the Roman alphabet and the Roman alphabet is lettering', he says.[1] His craftsmanship remains architectural although he never became an architect. His sculptures look as though they ought to have grown out of buildings rather than been stuck on to them, just as his book decorations intend to be typographic, that is, to grow out of the printed text. Neither his work nor his ideas are quite happy when standing alone. They must be related to something—a book or a building, a church, or God. Whatever reasons Morris gave for making beautiful things his real reason was to delight the senses. Eric Gill also believes that it is the business of art to please the senses, but he does not stop there. Sensibility is not enough. The art and the pleasure must be good: 'That is good art which pleases the senses as they ought to be pleased and the mind as it ought to be pleased.'[2] Neither is he content with an ethical generalization, however apposite. The moral conception of goodness is not enough. Goodness must be religious. 'God alone is good',[3] he says. And he resolves the problems of art by referring them back to moral or religious principles. Printing is put to the same test. In practice, however, it is not possible, at least in these times, to be consistently good in that strict sense.

'There are', he says, 'two typographies, as there are two worlds; and apart from God or profits, the test of one is mechanical perfection, and of the other sanctity—the commercial article at its best is simply physically serviceable and, *per accidens*, beautiful in its efficiency; the work of art at its best is

1 *An Essay on Typography* (2nd ed. 1936), 24.   2 *Beauty Looks After Herself* (1933), 27.   3 Ib. 15.

beautiful in its very substance and, *per accidens*, as serviceable as an article of commerce.'[1]

There is no doubt which of these two typographies he prefers and, although he is primarily out to serve God, he is prepared to serve Mammon in the form of the commercialism he abhors, on approved terms, namely by designing books and types which are serviceable in the commercial sense as distinct from the books and types which he designs to please the mind and the senses as they ought to be pleased. He will, in fact, remain in the world but not of it. And he is able to do so without serious hurt to his work or his conscience because he realizes that works of commerce and works of sanctity are destined to go on side by side (for long if not for ever), and that having two distinct objects and methods there is no reason why we should not help to cleanse the one whilst clinging to the other, industry 'becoming nobly utilitarian as it recognises its inherent limitations, and the world of human labour, ceasing any longer to compete with it, becoming more strictly and soberly humane'. It is a beneficent compromise born of a sense of fact. Eric Gill makes the best of two worlds by giving of his best to each, which is consistent with his belief that 'there is no happiness in a world in which things are not as good as they can be', and there can be few well-wishers of craftsmanship, and especially of typography, who do not welcome the honesty and clarity of the rules he has evolved for himself and applied so fastidiously.

Sometimes, however, he is a little hard on even a

1 *An Essay on Typography* (1931).

Title-page of Golden Cockerel Press edition of Chaucer's *Troilus and Criseyde.*

And whan that he was slayn in this manere
His lighte goost ful blisfully is went
Vp to the holwnesse of the eighte spere,
In conuers letyng euerich element :
And ther he saugh with ful auysement
The erratik sterres, herkenyng armonye
With sownes ful of heuenyssh melodie.

And down from thennes faste he gan auyse
This litel spot of erthe that with these
Enbraced is, and fully gan despise
This wrecched world, and held al vanite
To respect of the pleyn felicite
That is in heuene aboue. And at the laste,
Ther he was slayn his lokyng down he caste,

And in hymself he lough right at the wo
Of hem that wepen for his deth so faste,
And dampned al oure werk, that folwen so
The blynde lust the which that may nat laste,
And sholden al oure herte on heuene caste.
And forth he wente, shortly for to telle,
Ther as Mercurye sorted hym to dwelle.

Swich fyn hath tho this Troilus for loue,
Swich fyn hath al his grete worthynesse !
Swich fyn hath his estat real aboue !
Swich fyn his lust, swich fyn hath his noblesse !
Swich fyn this false worldes brotelnesse !
And thus bigan his louyng of Criseyde
As I haue told, and in this wise he deyde.

308

O Yonge fresshe folkes, he or she,
    In which ay loue vp groweth with youre age,
    Repeyreth hom fro worldly vanyte,
And of youre herte vp casteth the visage
To thilke god that after his ymage
Yow made; and thynketh al nys but a faire
This world, that passeth soone as floures faire!

And loueth hym, the which that righte for loue
Vpon a Crois, oure soules for to beye,
First starf, and roos, and sit in heuene aboue;
For he nyl falsen no wight, dar I seye,
That wol his herte al holly on hym leye!
And syn he best to loue is, and most meke,
What nedeth feyned loues for to seke?

Lo here, of payens corsed olde rites!
Lo here, what alle hire goddes may auaille!
Lo here, thise wrecched worldes appetites!
Lo here, the fyn and guerdoun for trauaille
Of Ioue, Appollo, of Mars, of swich rascaille!
Lo here, the forme of olde clerkes speche
In poetrie, if ye hire bokes seche!

O Moral Gower, this book I directe
    To the, and to the, Philosophical Strode,
    To vouchensauf, ther nede is, to correcte,
Of youre benignetes and zeles goode.
And to that sothfast Crist, that starf on rode,
With al myn herte, of mercy euere I preye,
And to the lord right thus I speke and seye:

corrupt industrialism. There can be no serious complaint when he says that 'Commercial printing, machine printing, industrial printing would have its own proper goodness if it were studiously plain and starkly efficient.' But his conditions begin to assume questionable shape when he pushes his logic so far as to demand that 'the typography of Industrialism' when it is 'not deliberately diabolical and designed to deceive', should not only be plain but that it should 'be wholly free from exuberance and fancy', because 'ornament is a kind of exuberance' and 'you cannot be exuberant by proxy'. Every sort of ornament, therefore, is to be renounced, for, he says, 'printers' flowers will not spring in an industrial soil, and fancy lettering is nauseating when it is not the fancy of typefounders and printers but simply of those who desire to make something appear better than it is'. It is obviously a counsel of perfection and therefore respectable, especially where it vetoes the use of devices to make things look better than they are. But Francis Meynell has proved that printers' flowers can show a pleasing and healthy growth both as books and advertisements 'in such a soil', and 'fancy lettering', even when it is the expression of a typefounder's or a printer's ebullience, irrespective of a desire for increased turnover, should not be encouraged, except in carefully chosen circumstances, and, as a matter of fact, it rarely is encouraged by Eric Gill, who has shown his sense of the value of simplicity in printing, and holds the commendable and courageous opinion that 'commonplace and normality' are 'essential to a good book-type'.[1]

[1] Introd. to 'SS. Perpetua and Felicity', *The Fleuron*, vii (1930).

On the other hand, he has many aphorisms which, if observed by industrialists, might conceivably help a mechanical commerce to behave itself. In the first place, as it is the aim of industry in a commercial age to be mechanical, all compromises are doomed to failure. 'It is not a question whether machine work be better than hand work—both have their proper goodness—it is simply a matter of difference . . . not all things made by machinery are bad things', nor is it true that 'the handicraftsman is the only kind of man that merits salvation. The industrialist is very welcome to all the credit he can get as a servant of humanity. The time has come when the handicraftsman should cease to rail at him or envy him. Let each go his own road.' He even goes so far as to say that, although the industrialist makes no claim to produce works of art, 'he does so nevertheless—when he is not imitating the works of the past'. And finally, whilst favouring simplicity in printing, Gill tolerantly leaves the door open for reasoning according to taste by the use of the concept 'pleasant'. After distinctiveness is achieved, 'pleasant reading is the compositor's main object'. What is pleasant is not stated, because perhaps so subjective a term is not amenable to definition. For him, characteristically, 'it involves first and last a consideration of what is holy'. But for the printer it means the discovery of the 'bounds of the virtue of haste . . . the bounds of the virtue of fancifulness . . . and above all they must collaborate to discover what is really pleasant in human life'. Even a convinced upholder of *laissez-faire* could face such principles with fortitude.

That being his attitude towards printing, how does he behave? The answer is, of course, to be found in his work. It is not what an artist says that matters so much as what he does, and what Eric Gill does as a craftsman or an artist is convincing, even though his dialectics and his theology may irritate or repel. His art is something more than a challenge: it is an achievement which manages to be both original and traditional, and, in so far as it is purposeful, and most of it has a purpose, it succeeds in being something as well as in doing something.

Gill left architecture for lettering. He carved letters in stone and drew them on paper and painted them on wood. It is a natural progress from lettering to printing. There are inherent relationships. In his case the recognition of those relationships was inevitable, for printing was the extension of an early passion for lettering, which he pursued as a child and perfected as a young man under the guidance of Edward Johnston; and the designing of type was a natural evolution for a printer who was also a letterer of genius. Twenty years ago he and a few friends started and operated the St. Dominic's Press at Ditchling in Sussex, from which issued many curious pamphlets and a small magazine, called *The Game* (1916–23), and his interest in printing continues professionally at the office of Hague & Gill in High Wycombe. His work as a typographer is also to be seen in the title-pages and books issued by a number of publishers in England and abroad, and notably in those produced in collaboration with Robert Gibbings at the Golden Cockerel Press. But whatever the operation or purpose, his attitude towards typography is predominatingly that of a letterer.

Gill never forgets that he is a letterer, and his type-faces, even after they have passed through the ordeal of mechanization, retain some of the sensitive qualities of

Cover of *The Game*, printed in red on brown paper, and first page. $7\frac{1}{4}'' \times 4\frac{7}{8}''$.

that craft. He always goes back to first principles and first causes, and his typography begins with the designing of the letter. Thus his printing is inclined to assert its lettered origins, as might be expected from one who is convinced that 'a good piece of lettering is as beautiful a thing to see as any sculpture or painted picture'.[1] He has got this enthusiasm into the pages of his books with the result that the type is sometimes disconcertingly self-important. Gill's lay-out is often restless, but it is possible to forget it; it is possible also (rather surprisingly) to

[1] *An Essay on Typography* (2nd ed. 1936), 122.

forget his unregistered right-hand margins, but it is difficult to become unconscious of his types.

He is so enamoured of lettering and so conscious of its origin and purposes that he has lately come to the conclusion that it should no longer be associated with print-

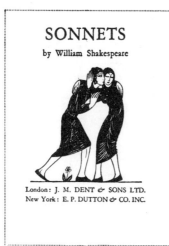

Title-page of *Sonnets*: The Temple Shakespeare. 4″ × 5⅛″.

Cover of booklet printed at St. Dominic's Press, Ditchling. 4¾″ × 3⅝″.

ing. 'Lettering', he says, 'has had its day. Spelling, and philology, and all such pedantries have no place in our world. The only way to reform modern lettering is to abolish it.[1]' He argues that the book of the future should be printed in shorthand, which he considers to be more suitable for modern mechanical conditions.

This, however, is a dip into a future where eccentricity has plenty of room to flap its wings, and in the meantime it may be presumed that typography will have his more normal services in the old tradition, for it is as a

1 *An Essay on Typography* (2nd ed. 1936), 133.

designer of types rather than of books that Gill has most influenced modern typography. His habit of innovation by throwing back to the primitive and the archaic has not as yet been imitated, nor is there any likelihood of

18

SHALL I compare thee to a Summers day?
Thou art more lovely and more temperate:
Rough windes do shake the darling buds of Maie,
And Sommers lease hath all too short a date:
Sometime too hot the eye of heaven shin:es,
And often is his gold complexion dimm'd,
And every faire from faire some-time declines,
By chance, or natures changing course untrim'd:
But thy eternall Sommer shall not fade,
Nor loose possession of that faire thou ow'st,
Nor shall death brag thou wandr'st in his shade,
When in eternall lines to time thou grow'st,
So long as men can breath or eyes can see,
So long lives this, and this gives life to thee.

19

DEVOURING time blunt thou the Lyons pawes,
And make the earth devoure her owne sweet brood,
Plucke the keene teeth from the fierce Tygers jawes,
And burne the long liv'd Phœnix in her blood,
Make glad and sorry seasons as thou fleet'st,
And do what ere thou wilt swift-footed time
To the wide world and all her fading sweets:
But I forbid thee one most hainous crime,
O carve not with thy howers my loves faire brow,
Nor draw noe lines there with thine antique pen,
Him in thy course untainted doe allow,
For beauties patterne to succeding men.
Yet doe thy worst ould Time dispight thy wrong,
My love shall in my verse ever live young.

Opening of *Shakespeare's Sonnets*, edited by Margaret Flower, typography and type by Eric Gill. $6\frac{1}{2}'' \times 4\frac{1}{8}''$.

such individual preferences as no title-page (as in the first edition of the *Essay on Typography*), or a combined title and contents page (as in the second edition), or the unregistered right-hand edges of his lines, being widely adopted, any more than there is an indication that a specially designed text italic, such as Joanna, will be demanded by readers of poetry.[1]

His aim both as a letterer and a typographer is always

1 Gill's Joanna italic was first used for an entire book in Margaret Flower's edition of Shakespeare's *Sonnets* (Cassell & Co., Ltd., 1933).

'to discover the norm', and this consistent throwing back, or digging down, has been of great value especially in the realm of type-faces,[1] where, with the intelligent co-operation of the Monotype Corporation, he has had a good influence more widespread than could otherwise have been possible. As a designer of types he has been an adapter rather than an inventor, the invention of a new type being next to impossible. But there is distinct originality in his treatment of a text italic in his Joanna, and he has made Perpetua his own much as Edward FitzGerald added *Omar Khayyám* to the treasury of English poetry; whilst he has given grace and proportion to the most bleakly functional of all types. The Gill Sans types are an inevitable consequence of functionalism or mechanical design, and quite naturally they have become the predominant modern commercial typographical characters. It is one of Gill's most emphatic rules that design for mechanical production must be free from ornamentation, and he has successfully pushed this idea to its logical conclusion in the Sans series. 'Mechanised man', he says, 'knows no fancy and curved serifs and such like refinements, dependent as they must be upon the sensibilities of the man who makes them, are rightly to be eschewed by those who design things for machine facture.'[2] He believes, however, that serifs are a useful adjunct to letters, and it might be argued that he designed the Sans series to put mechanized printing in its proper

1 Eric Gill is responsible for four new (or newly designed) type-faces: 1. Joanna Roman. 2. Joanna Italic. 3. Perpetua. 4. Gill Sans.   2 *A Specimen of Three Book Types designed by Eric Gill: Joanna, Joanna Italic, Perpetua* (1934), Preface.

place. He blames machine printing for still being medieval and incapable of supplying 'a plain job'. The master printer is not a printer but a salesman who refuses to do a plain job of work because it is not good business.

Within the reproduced facsimile:

30   An Essay on Typography

at an angle, as in the K. The letter-cutter naturally avoids such things. ¶ Again, take the letter G. The evolution of our modern small g is seen to be chiefly due to the prevalence of & consequent familiarity with hastily scribbled forms (see fig. 3). Nevertheless, in no case does the scribe imagine he is inventing a new form: he is only concerned to make well or ill the form with which he is familiar.

¶ By the sixth century a form of writing obviously more natural to penmanship (see British Museum Harl. MS. 1775) had been evolved. And the process continued until all resemblance to the Roman original was hidden (see B. M. Add. MS. 24585). ¶ I am not concerned to describe in detail the history of the process in its technical and economic significance. The point that chiefly concerns me is that, with whatever tools or materials or economic circumstance (that is hurry & expense), the artist, the letter-maker, has always thought of himself as making existing forms, & not inventing new ones. Thus, the Lombards of the fourteenth century did not sit down and invent Lombardic lettering. The Siennese inscription in the Victoria and Albert Museum, dated 1309, is simply a stone version of the pen letters with which the letter-cutter was fami-

(Figure 3(1-8) shows the evolution of the lower-case g from the Roman original. 9-11 are comic modern varieties having more relation to pairs of spectacles than to lettering — as though the designer had said A pair of spectacles is rather like a g; I will make a g rather like a pair of spectacles.)

liar. The letter-cutters of the fifteenth century did not invent 'gothic'. They had the job of cutting stone inscriptions, and they did it in the ordinary letters of their time. The forms of their letters were what we call 'pen' forms. But they cared nothing about that. To them they were simply letters. And just as we saw that in Roman times the Roman scribe imitated the stone inscription forms be-

Opening of Eric Gill's *Essay on Typography*. $6\frac{3}{4}'' \times 4''$.

'It won't sell because it won't tickle any buyer's fancy', but this, he is careful to point out, is not a peculiarity of the printing trade. 'To get anything really plain is very difficult, but in the trade of book printing it is as yet impossible.' But his objection is only to mechanical ornamentation and faked fancifulness. Decoration and ornament are the province of the artist not of the gadget-ruled business man.

He has contributed definite characteristics to typographical design, as well as to the designing of types, and, exotic as some of his designs seem to be, they have not only a firm link with the past but a reasoned relationship with the present. He has courageously faced the problem of the mass-production of books and hammered out for himself and others rules which are logically derived from the needs of the reader. He does not set out to make a book beautiful but a book useful, believing that beauty will take care of itself if the rules of honest and considerate production are followed. 'The things which should form the shape and proportion of the page', he says, 'are the hand and the eye.'[1] The ordinary commercial editions of his own essays, particularly the second edition of the *Essay on Typography*, and the new *Temple Shakespeare*, show how distinction and convenience can meet even on business grounds if there is good taste and honesty on both sides.

AN ESSAY ON TYPOGRAPHY
BY ERIC GILL

Contents:

second edition
LONDON / SHEED & WARD / 1936

Combined title-page and contents page. $6\frac{3}{4}'' \times 4''$.

1 *An Essay on Typography* (1936), 108.

XI

FRANCIS MEYNELL

IN THE PROSPECTUS OF THE FIRST BOOK IN THE FIRST NONE-
such *List* (1923) there is a sentence which, by implication,
promises what Francis Meynell was to achieve. It comes
at the end of a glowing but not exaggerated anticipation
of the *Love Poems of John Donne*. 'This is a remarkably
beautiful volume', it says, 'to be treasured by book
collectors as well as by those who use books for reading.'
The implications are important, for they promise to
gratify the whims of the collector and the needs of the
reader. The words may have seemed to swagger a little,
but looking back at them any such seeming has been
wiped out by fulfilment. The novelty of the statement
was not the brag but the promise to remember the reader
whilst looking after the interests of the collector, 'to
produce books', as the Prospectus of 1931 said, 'which
are indeed books, not toys; for admiration certainly, but
for reading, for reference, for the elucidation of textual
problems, and for hard wear'. The work of designing
the Nonesuch books begins with the text, as all books
made for the authentic reader must, with the result that
the reprints of classical works issued by the press are as
distinguished for their scholarship as they are for their
typography.

A printer who had already proved that he could design
books thus announces his willingness to make reading the
chief test of the success of his designs. It is significant,
and possibly inevitable also, that the man who made that

statement, and who was to become the most versatile of all designers of books, should have reached his trade by way of literature rather than printing.

Francis Meynell had the good luck, or as Samuel Butler would have said, the cunning, to be born into a family of readers and writers. His mother was Alice Meynell, the poet and essayist; his father, Wilfred Meynell, an editor and publisher of distinction. Their home was a magnet for men of letters, and, for a time, the abode also of another poet, Francis Thompson, and a congenial meeting-place for authors of the rank of Coventry Patmore, George Meredith, Wilfred Scawen Blunt, and W. B. Yeats. Francis and his brothers and sisters throve in this exalted atmosphere. They read and composed prose and poetry when other children would be playing at Indians, and Francis records that he drank tea out of the tea-pot which had poured for Robert Browning, pocketed 'a yearly tip of a pound at Christmas' from George Meredith, and at the age of seven declaimed Gray's *Elegy* from beneath the table at which the Sunday night supper guests sat.

This 'literary hot-house' might have produced in him 'an over-sensitive literary plant', but, instead of making a poet, 'letters', he says, 'made me into a printer'. This is an understatement. He is far more than a printer, far more even than a good printer. We have had, and still have, many good printers. But until recent years we have lacked men with the ambition as well as the taste and skill to design a succession of books admirable in all their parts and successful within the conventions of trade and under the conditions of mechanical production. The idea of a book as an organism was not new, as readers of this work are aware, and although the methods of Francis Meynell are very different from those of William Morris, Charles Ricketts, or St. John Hornby, without the example of those typographical idealists the task of the Nonesuch Press would have been more difficult. There are several printers as good as Francis Meynell, but there are few designers of books worthy to stand near him for quality or technique, and none so versatile, not only in book-printing, for he has produced or designed almost every kind of ephemeral printed matter from labels and bill-heads to hand-bills, folders, pamphlets, and periodicals.

If he had designed nothing but the impressive and entertaining series of *Nonesuch Lists* and *Prospectuses* he would have been distinguished among printers. These admirable pamphlets and their attendant leaflets, unequalled and unsurpassed in their class, set a new standard for publishers' advertisements in quality of paper, variety, and attractiveness of design, as well as in wittiness of text.

Francis Meynell has a genius for making opulent, even bizarre, materials serve a useful purpose. He is at the head of his craft as a book-designer because he knows how to blend format and text, and he has been successful in doing so because he has accepted full responsibility for the choice of his books and their appearance. He has thrown back to the methods of the printer-publishers who reached their height in England with the magnificent

REPRINTED FROM "THE DAILY NEWS AND LEADER." OF 14 AUGUST, 1917

A REASONABLE MAN'S PEACE

BY H. G. WELLS

THE international situation at the present time is beyond question the most wonderful that the world has ever seen. There is not a country in the world in which the great majority of sensible people is not passionately desirous of peace, of an enduring peace, and—the war goes on.

The conditions of peace can now be stated in general terms that are as acceptable to a reasonable man in Berlin as they are to a reasonable man in Paris or London or Petrograd or Constantinople. There are to be no conquests, no domination of recalcitrant populations, no bitter insistence upon vindictive penalties, and there must be something in the nature of a world-wide League of Nations to keep the peace securely in future, to "make the world safe for democracy" and maintain international justice. To that the general mind of the world has come to-day.

Why, then, does the waste and killing go on? Why is not the Peace Conference sitting now?

Manifestly because a small minority of people in positions of peculiar advantage, in positions of trust and authority, prevent or delay its assembling.

The answer which seems to suffice in all the Allied countries is that the German Imperial Government, that the German Imperial Government alone, stands in the way, that its tradition is incurably a tradition of conquest and aggression, that until German militarism is overthrown, &c. Few people in the Allied countries will dispute that that is broadly true. But is it the whole and complete truth? Is there nothing more to be done on our side? Let us put a question that goes to the very heart of the problem. Why does the great mass of the German people still cling to its incurably belligerent Government?

The answer to that question is not overwhelmingly difficult. The German people sticks to its militarist imperialism as Mazeppa stuck to his horse: because it is bound to it and the wolves pursue. The attentive student of the home and foreign propaganda literature of the German Government will realise that the case made by German imperialism, the main argument by which it sticks to power, is this, that the Allied Governments are also imperialist, that they also aim at conquest and aggression, that for Germany the choice is world-empire or downfall and utter ruin. This is the argument that holds the German people stiffly united. For most men in most countries it would be a convincing argument, strong enough

First page of 4 pp. War leaflet, designed by Francis Meynell for the Pelican Press, 1917. $8\frac{3}{4}'' \times 5\frac{5}{8}''$.

enterprises of John Baskerville, Jacob Tonson, and Bernard Lintot in the eighteenth century, and who faded out as a commercial class in the early nineteenth. From the first his aim was not solely to print with particular regard for his own taste and that of the reader of taste, but to plan and control the production of 'a whole book—text, editor and artist, as well as paper-maker and binder'.

He was well placed for such an adventure, for his earliest experience in affairs was connected with books in the publishing house of Burns & Oates, of which firm his father was managing director, and he had 'a hand in designing' the *Collected Works of Francis Thompson*. That was in 1913, and in the same year he met Stanley Morison, 'who had just emerged from a bank and was anxious to concern himself with book-production', and got his first chance in the book world in the same publishing house. There is little to distinguish Francis Meynell's early typographical work from that of any good printing of the time, but in 1914 he went a step farther towards evolving a technique for himself. Once more he helped himself out of the stores of the past. He bought a hand-press and set it up in his dining-room at 67 Romney Street, Westminster (the birthplace of English printing), and with Fell types bought (by special favour) from the Delegates of the University Press, Oxford, began printing for the first time under his own house flag. Two books appear with the imprint of the Romney Street Press, but, although prentice-work, they show a ripeness in taste and technique indicating a genius for that sort of thing which needed only time

TEN POEMS
BY ALICE MEYNELL
1913—1915

WESTMINSTER
THE ROMNEY STREET PRESS
1915

Title-page of *Ten Poems by Alice Meynell*, printed by Francis Meynell on the
Romney Street Press, Westminster. $8\frac{7}{8}'' \times 6\frac{3}{4}''$.

and experience to express itself in masterpieces.[1] His apprenticeship was expedited by meeting Bruce Rogers, 'inspirer of all eager young typographers', and George Lansbury who found the capital which enabled him to start the Pelican Press and inaugurate a new era in commercial printing.

When Francis Meynell (supported by Vera Mendel and David Garnett) launched the Nonesuch Press in 1923 opportunity and the man were well met. Witty men and men of taste had often set their mark upon the printing of books, but never before had a printer and publisher arisen who combined wit and taste with business acumen. Francis Meynell has taste and wit in all his sayings and doings, and, although a business man, he is something more, because he refuses to make profit by sweating the quality of his product. But in addition to these more or less safe qualities he has a revolutionary streak of audacity, otherwise the Nonesuch would not have existed or its books would have been less adventurous than they are. Everything about the enterprise was audacious: its obscure origin in a Soho cellar; its unusual range of printers, authors, artists, editors, types, papers, bindings, formats, and prices. And still more audacious the bending of machines and trade printing to the purposes of art and scholarship for the delight and advantage of readers.

The aim of the Nonesuch as set out in the first *List* was 'to choose and make books according to a triple ideal: significance of subject, beauty of format, and moderation of price'. And twelve years later the intention was stated

1 See Notes, pp. 278–9, *infra*.

BUTLERIANA

1932

THE NONESUCH PRESS
16 Great James Street
Bloomsbury

Title-page of the Nonesuch *Butleriana.* 9⅛″ × 5⅜″.

THE WORKS OF

SHAKESPEARE

The text of the First Folio with
Quarto variants and a selection
of modern readings: edited
by Herbert Farjeon

★

THE TEMPEST

THE TWO GENTLEMEN OF VERONA

THE MERRY WIVES OF WINDSOR

MEASURE FOR MEASURE

THE COMEDIE OF ERRORS

MUCH ADOE ABOUT NOTHING

LOVES LABOUR'S LOST

THE NONESUCH PRESS

NEW YORK: RANDOM HOUSE INC.

MCMXXIX

Title-page of the Nonesuch *Shakespeare*. $9\frac{1}{2}'' \times 5\frac{9}{10}''$.

HOMER
THE ILIAD
POPE

THE NONESUCH PRESS MCMXXXI

Title-page of the Nonesuch *Homer*. $10\frac{4}{5}'' \times 6''$.

more concretely: 'Our stock-in-trade has been the theory that mechanical means could be made to serve fine ends; that the machine in printing was a controllable tool. Therefore we set out to be mobilisers of other people's resources; to be designers, specifiers, rather than manufacturers; architects of books rather than builders.'[1]

In the earliest days of printing, design was good because the printer imitated the manuscript which he supplanted. Respect for the method has survived. The members of the Roxburghe Club, for instance, went into ecstasies over what they called 'the black-letter', and a hundred years later William Morris actually inaugurated a new era of printing by emulating the methods of Caxton.

Francis Meynell owns allegiance to no particular period or tradition, although he has a pronounced liking for the literature of the seventeenth century, as well as its types and formats which he has adapted to modern needs.[2] But he roves over many periods, and his sensitiveness to the needs of the modern reader protects him from antiquarianism. He so transmutes his pilferings that the past becomes the present, and he is aware of his processes. This is made clear at an early stage, as the following extract from the prospectus of the *Love Poems of John Donne* proves:

'The Nonesuch Press edition is printed in the unique 17th century Fell types. The typographical flavour of the book, it will be seen, is that of Donne's own day. In one trifling respect only has this type been altered; we mention it as an indication

1 See Notes, pp. 279–80, *infra.*   2 More than thirty of the first hundred Nonesuch books were written or translated in the seventeenth century and no less than seven of the first eight announced in 1923.

of the watchful care which the Press takes of its own work even down to the last comma—literally. For the comma is too heavy in the Fell type, and a new one has been designed for this book. . . . This is the first book to be printed in Fell italics, of which so little exists that one sheet of the text has had to be machined and the type distributed before the next could be composed.'

Another instance of care for the reader is in the *Poems of Andrew Marvell*, which, according to the prospectus, 'follows the unique British Museum copy page for page, line for line, word for word, spelling for spelling, style for style', but, it is important to observe, 'in a smaller size, more convenient for use than the over-large folio with the over-large type of the original . . . it is a facsimile as regards text and arrangement; but, while generous in its proportions, it is set in a type more charming and in a format easier on the hands, the shelf and the purse, than the original edition'.[1]

A less versatile designer might easily have produced a new uniformity; or he might have become addicted to the commercial superstition of change for the sake of change—and the hope of profit! Books are exposed to both these risks. Nor is the danger removed when their production is under the control of an artist, for few artists have more than one or two tricks.

Those who bring rabbits or guinea-pigs out of hats rarely enliven us by producing marmosets or budgerigars. With Francis Meynell the magic hat becomes a lucky bag. Every dip produces a surprise. Most inventive of typographers, he keeps his admirers on their toes won-

[1] *First List of Nonesuch Books* (1923).

dering what he will be up to next. He has, in fact, made book-production an entertainment as well as an adventure. We enjoy the Nonesuch books and feel certain that their inventor enjoyed himself in their production. He has proved that it is possible for printing to be earnest without being serious. Typography as he practises it is a joyful science. His technique suggests the discipline of a game rather than that of a reformation, so that on the appearance of successive Nonesuch masterpieces you can almost hear the fervent 'Well played, Sir!' of the devotee.

To have remained a printer-publisher would have crabbed his style, so while retaining a hand-press of his own, for experimental and occasional work, he abandoned the idea of printing his own publications and enlisted into his service no less than twenty-two presses of this country with occasional recruitments from overseas.[1] Twenty-six different type faces were used for the hundred works produced during the years 1923–34, each one of which has a different format. This achievement, novel and astonishing in itself, enabled him to tap most of the best sources of modern printing at a time when a new typographical impulsion was beginning to bear fruit. The Nonesuch is as much a focus of this revival of

[1] The presses used include A. Alexander, Bishop & Garrett, William Brendon & Sons, Cambridge University Press, Camelot Press, Chiswick Press, Richard Clay & Sons, R. & R. Clark, T. & A. Constable, Curwen Press, Dura Press, Enschadé, Fanfare Press, Geo. Gibbons, Daniel Jacomet, A. W. Jones, Kynoch Press, Lowe & Brydon, R. Maclehose, Oxford University Press, Pelican Press, Westminster Press. Two books, *The Temple* by George Herbert and Beedome's *Poems*, have been printed on the Nonesuch Press itself.

good trade-printing under modern mechanical conditions, and as much an act of co-ordination, as it is a work of individual typographical expression. Francis Meynell's control of the machine has been excellently

DEDICATION
*If the printer has any right
of dedication, then:*
TO
LILIAS
and to ROBERT *in prison*

THE PRINTER TO
THE READER

A manuscript Note Book of the time of the Commonwealth, written in very charming characters, bound in contemporary covers of blue velvet, was lately found by Ev. M. in the sixpenny pile of a bookstall. It is from among the contents of this Note Book that I have chosen the passages now printed. The spelling has been modernised, as the easiest way (but, I admit, by no means the best) of securing uniformity where none existed. The order of the several pieces is not that of composition (all but one are dated) but of the

Opening page of *Meditations from the Note Book of Mary Carey, 1649–1657.* Printed by Francis Meynell on the Romney Street Press, Westminster, 1918. $5\frac{1}{2}'' \times 3\frac{1}{4}''$.

summed up by A. J. A. Symons, himself a notable typographer, in his *Appraisal* of the Nonesuch Press:[1]

'It is due to him, more than to any other man, that, in printing at least, the nettle of the machine has been grasped in our time. He has shown, not once, but fifty times, that the super-

---

[1] *The Nonesuch Century: An Appraisal, a Personal Note and a Bibliography of the First Hundred Books issued by the Press, 1923–1934.* By A. J. A. Symons, Francis Meynell, and Desmond Flower (1936). All the quotations in this chapter, unless otherwise stated, are taken from this work.

session of hand manufacture by machine making, which is obviously to be the rule of our life henceforward in most, if not all, of its material activities, need leave us no misgivings if we can adapt our intelligence to machine-control.'

In the general appraisal of these books there are, of course, points of disagreement, and even of disapproval. But the masterpieces of the series are rarely if ever challenged. I have yet to meet any one, for instance, who would not give first place to the *Shakespeare*, for here dignity of format and scholarly, or perhaps it might be better to say common-sense, editing have made a book which is good to see, to handle, and to read.

Opinions about books, as about other things, vary with attitude, and the choice of the book-fancier may differ from that of the reader. But though readership is the aim of authorship, only a minority of readers care particularly for the physical condition of their books; and although a plain or even a shabby garment does not detract from the golden word, the wide acceptance of the Nonesuch books proves that typophilia and bibliophilia may be on good terms. The reason is that, being a reader himself and coming of good literary stock, Francis Meynell, even in his most adventurous moments, rarely forgets the reader. That is not to say that the Nonesuch books are a hundred per cent excellent. Homer sometimes nods. But even the failures are interesting, much as a failure to kick a goal or win a race may be interesting.[1]

[1] Francis Meynell has favourites among his publications and in an interview printed in the *Observer*, November 19th, 1933, he confessed to having particular pleasure in the three-volume *Blake*, the *Shakespeare*, and the 'various small books of John Evelyn, the Diarist, which had never before been printed'.

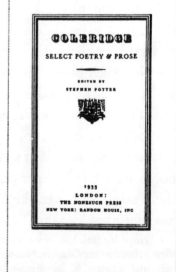

Opening of the Nonesuch *Izaak Walton*. $8\frac{1}{2}'' \times 5\frac{1}{16}''$.

Title-page of Thomas Beedome's *Poems*, Nonesuch Press. $7\frac{9}{10}'' \times 4\frac{7}{10}''$.

Title-page of the Nonesuch *Coleridge* in the Compendious Series. $7\frac{7}{8}'' \times 4\frac{1}{2}''$.

My attitude is that of a reader: of a reader who, in spite of his liking for a handsome book, shares a preference for beauty unadorned, with a tenderness for well-read shabbiness. It is a catholic taste, and among the Nonesuch treasures it ranges appreciatively from the austere and appropriate *Milton* and the companionable *Walton* to the period quaintness of Thomas Beedome's *Select Poems* and the pocketable elegance of *Pindar*. On the other hand, my chief antipathy is not for the over-decorated *Book of Ruth*, which, despite the opulence of its Geofrey Tory borders and the publisher's admission that it had 'been made essentially for collectors of curious printing',[1] is a readable as well as a seductive piece of confectionery, but for *The Anatomy of Melancholy*. And here the objection is editorial, not typographical. This handsome edition attracts book-collectors rather than Burtonians, for one reason because Burton's marginal notes and footnotes have been omitted and the text has been decorated. I don't want to be told that McKnight Kauffer's illustrations are works of genius: I know that already; or even that they are 'significant commentations' on the text, which is a matter of opinion. To Burtonians the original annotations are essential and any illustrations are otiose. Imagine the text of the Nonesuch *Shakespeare* broken with graphic interpretations or comments by— anybody! Yet here I find myself in a dilemma, because two of my favourites, the *Milton* and the *Dante*, are illustrated.[2] It may be that Blake and Botticelli blend

1 *First List of Nonesuch Books.*   2 *Milton* by William Blake and *Dante* by Botticelli.

better with epic poetry than the decorations of the
Anatomy with seventeenth-century psychology. Perhaps
Botticelli and Blake are nearer to Dante and Milton than
McKnight Kauffer to Burton. Perhaps it is because they
illustrate while they decorate, and although poetry may
in unique circumstances such as these be illustrated,
science should never be decorated. At the same time I
prefer my Shakespeare plain, I can enjoy Blake's illustrations of *Milton* and Botticelli's of *Dante* apart from
Milton or *Dante*.[1]

But when you have exhausted your praise and ventured
a diffident criticism or two, and looked back at the full
Nonesuch record there is little of it you would alter, but
since a purpose is consoling there is comfort in the
thought that the books are at their best when they
approximate to the needs of the common reader, and,
generally speaking, they do so less in the limited editions,
especially in the more spectacular of them, than in those
'compendious' volumes representing such writers as
Blake, Swift, Hazlitt, Donne, and William Morris. I
may look admiringly at the others but these are the books
I read. They are elegant in design, friendly in format,
adequately edited, and accessible to the moderate purse.
Need a book be more?

1 Francis Meynell is fully aware of this problem of the illustrator, who,
he rightly believes, should be a commentator rather than a decorator.
'Kauffer on Burton' is how he would describe the drawings for the Nonesuch edition of the *Anatomy*. See *The Nonesuch Century*, 44.

PART III

OCCASIONAL PAPERS

I

THE TYPOGRAPHY OF WILLIAM MORRIS[1]

WILLIAM MORRIS IS AN IRONIC FIGURE. HIS ACHIEVEMENTS not only missed their mark, but hit marks he was not aiming at. His printing is no exception. The master-pieces of the Kelmscott Press which he aimed at making 'useful pieces of goods' were typographical curiosities from birth, and so far removed from the common way of readers that they have become models of what a book should not be.

He was a Bibliophile, or more exactly, a typophile whose affections became unruly in the presence of decorated incunabula, and, although he was outwardly correct towards pure printing, his heart was not there. According to Sir Sydney Cockerell he flirted with the idea of a folio edition of *The Earthly Paradise*, 'profusely illustrated by Sir Edward Burne-Jones', a quarter of a century before the inception of the Kelmscott Press. His personal taste was much the same then as later, although he continued to pay homage to good as distinct from fine printing. It was the 'essence of my undertaking', he said, 'to produce books which it would be a pleasure to look upon as pieces of printing and arrangement of type'. Thus inspired by the example of 'the calligraphy of the Middle Ages, and the earlier printing which took its place', and in spite of his passion for decorated books he observed that the early printed

1 A paper read at the William Morris Centenary Dinner of the Double Crown Club at the Café Royal, May 2nd, 1934.

books 'were always beautiful by force of the mere typography, even without the added ornament with which
many of them are so lavishly supplied'.

Much has been made of the emphasis he laid upon the
book as an organic assembly of paper, type, and binding.
But although few printers or publishers in the nineteenth
century had insisted upon the excellence of these ingredients, as he did, the architectonic principle had never
been wholly ignored. But in the main it was unconsciously observed. Deliberation is evident in the construction of the Pickering books, in the Keepsakes and
Table Books of the thirties and forties, in the illustrated
books of the sixties, and the later productions of the
Daniel Press; and, if we may leave England for a moment,
in such convenient publications as those of Bernhard
Tauchnitz, where there is rectitude to satisfy the demands
of the most austere of functionalists.

It was not, then, the architectonics of the Kelmscott
books which evoked a typographical revolution. Nor
was it the pursuit of beauty which always haunted
Morris's intentions. 'I began printing books', he said,
'in the hope of producing some which would have a
definite claim to beauty.' Many printers and publishers
of the time would have claimed as much. Bad taste
in the arts and crafts is invariably the result of beauty-
mongering, and the more costly books of the nineteenth
century are littered with beauty from cover to cover.

Neither was it originality. Morris never sought to be
original. He was a revivalist, and all his work is derivative.
There is nothing new even in that, for all the arts and

crafts are derivative, and originality is apt to be a myth and often a nuisance. Morris was even less original than many other earnest innovators, and the Kelmscott books are derivatives twice removed. They are modern variations of the early printed books of northern Europe, as they in turn were but mechanical imitations of the manuscripts which preceded the invention of movable types.

Nor again was there anything peculiar even in that, for all mechanical evolution seems to proceed in the same manner. The earliest railway carriages followed the lines of the stage-coach; the earliest steamships were schooners and brigantines with funnels and paddle-boxes; and the earliest motor-car was a horseless-carriage complete with tail-board. It is not surprising to learn that the earliest printed books were imitations of manuscripts, but it is surprising to find a nineteenth-century printer of genius imitating the imitations.

There is, however, more than one difference between these mechanical devices and the Kelmscott books. The engineers copied because they could not think of anything better. Now and then they even made concessions to beauty, in the form of superadded decorations, much as Morris did. But there was a marked difference between them, for Morris knew better. Although to him beauty meant decoration or ornament, yet in the first edition of *The Roots of the Mountains* he actually produced an undecorated book of great distinction. The book is not only admirable in itself, but it has had a better influence on recent typography than all the Kelmscott books together. Morris himself was delighted with the book.

THE ROOTS OF THE MOUNTAINS WHEREIN IS TOLD SOMEWHAT OF THE LIVES OF THE MEN OF BURG DALE THEIR FRIENDS THEIR NEIGHBOURS THEIR FOEMEN AND THEIR FELLOWS IN ARMS BY WILLIAM MORRIS

WHILES CARRIED O'ER THE IRON ROAD.
WE HURRY BY SOME FAIR ABODE ;
THE GARDEN BRIGHT AMIDST THE HAY,
THE YELLOW WAIN UPON THE WAY,
THE DINING MEN, THE WIND THAT SWEEPS
LIGHT LOCKS FROM OFF THE SUN-SWEET HEAPS—
THE GABLE GREY, THE HOARY ROOF,
HERE NOW—AND NOW SO FAR ALOOF.
HOW SORELY THEN WE LONG TO STAY
AND MIDST ITS SWEETNESS WEAR THE DAY,
AND 'NEATH ITS CHANGING SHADOWS SIT,
AND FEEL OURSELVES A PART OF IT.
SUCH REST, SUCH STAY, I STROVE TO WIN
WITH THESE SAME LEAVES THAT LIE HEREIN.

LONDON MDCCCXC : REEVES AND TURNER
CXCVI STRAND

Title-page of *The Roots of the Mountains*, first edition. Designed by William Morris
$7\frac{1}{4}'' \times 5\frac{3}{8}''$.

When Adam delved and Eve span,
who was then the gentleman?

A DREAM OF JOHN BALL.

CHAPTER I.

THE MEN OF KENT.

SOMETIMES I am rewarded for fretting myself so much about present matters by a quite unasked-for pleasant dream. I mean when I am asleep. This dream is as it were a present of an architectural peep-show. I see some beautiful and noble building new made, as it were for the occasion, as clearly as if I were awake; not vaguely or absurdly, as often happens in dreams, but with all the detail clear and reasonable. Some Elizabethan house with its scrap of earlier fourteenth-century building, and its later degradations of Queen Anne and Silly Billy and Victoria, marring but not destroying it, in an old village once a clearing amid the sandy woodlands of Sussex. Or an old and unusually curious church, much church-wardened, and beside it a fragment of fifteenth-century domestic architecture amongst the not unpicturesque lath and plaster of an Essex farm,

A Dream of John Ball, first edition. Frontispiece by Burne Jones, and first page. 6½″ × 5″.

'Now must ye wayfarers depart; for the road is but rough, and the day not over-long.'

Then she turned to Face-of-god and put her hand on his shoulder, and brought her face close to his and spake to him softly: 'Doth this second parting seem at all strange to thee, and that I am now so familiar to thee, I whom thou didst once deem to be a very goddess? And now thou hast seen me grow pale with fear because of thee; and thou hast felt my caresses which I might not refrain; even as if I were altogether such a maiden as ye warriors hang about for a nine days' wonder, and then all is over save an aching heart—wilt thou do so with me? Tell me, have I not belittled myself before thee as if I asked thee to scorn me? For thus desire dealeth both with maid and man.'

He said : 'In all this there is but one thing for me to say, and that is that I love thee; and surely none the less, but rather the more, because thou lovest me, and art of my kind, and mayest share in my deeds and think well of them. Now is my heart full of joy, and one thing only weigheth on it; and that is that my kinswoman the Bride begrudgeth our love together. For this is the thing that of all things most misliketh me, that any should bear a grudge against me.'

She said : 'Forget not the token, and my message to her.'

'I will not forget it,' said he. 'And now I bid thee to kiss me even before all these that are looking on ; for there is nought so belittle us therein, since we be troth-plight.'

And indeed those folk stood all round about them gazing on them, but a little aloof, that they might not hear their words if they were minded to talk privily. For they had long loved the Sun-beam, and now the love of Face-of-god had begun to spring up in their hearts.

So the twain embraced and kissed one another, and made no haste thereover ; and those men deemed that but meet and right, and clashed their weapons on their shields in token of their joy.

150

Then Face-of-god turned about and strode out of the ring of men, with Bow-may and Wood-wise beside him, and they went on their journey over the necks towards Burgstead. But the Sun-beam turned slowly from that place toward the Vale, and two of the stoutest carles went along with her to guard her from harm, and she went down into the Vale pondering all these things in her heart.

Then the other earles dragged off the corpses of the Dusky Men till they had brought them to the sheer necks above the Shivering Flood, and there they tossed them over into the boiling caldron of the force, and so departed talking with them the silver arm-rings of the slain to add to the tale.

But when they came back into the Vale the Sun-beam duly ordered that watch and ward to keep the ingate thereto, and note all that should befall till Folk-might came home.

CHAPTER XXII. FACE-OF-GOD COMETH HOME TO BURGSTEAD.

BUT Face-of-god with Bow-may and Wood-wise fared over the waste, going at first alongside the cliffs of the Shivering Flood, and then afterwards turning somewhat to the west. They soon had to climb a very high and steep bent going up to a mountain-neck ; and the way over the neck was rough indeed when they were on it, and they toiled out of it into a barren valley, and out of the valley again on to a rough neck ; and such-like was their journey the day long, for they were going ashwart all those great gret dykes that went from the ice-mountains toward the lower dales like the outspread fingers of a hand or the roots of a great tree. And the ice-mountains they had on their left hands and whiles at their backs.

They went very warily, with their bows bended and spear in hand, but saw no man, good or bad, and but few living things.

151

Departum from Shadony Vale.

Opening, *The Roots of the Mountains.* 7¼″ × 5⅜″.

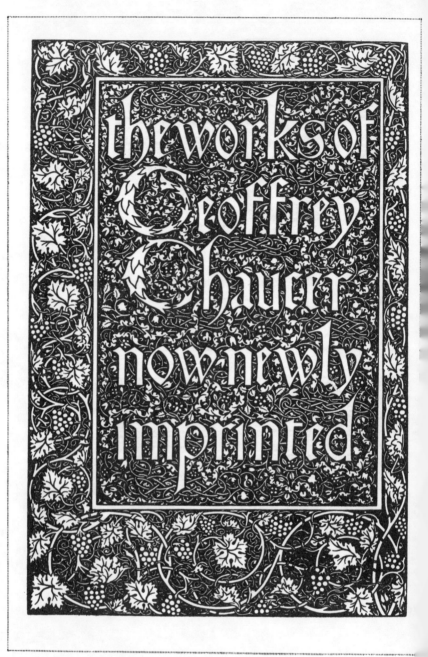

Title-page of the Kelmscott *Chaucer*. Type and decoration by William Morris. $16\frac{3}{4}'' \times 11\frac{1}{4}''$.

And to a dronke man the wey is slider;
And certes in this world so faren we,
We seken faste after felicitee,
But we goon wrong ful often trewely.
Thus may we seyen alle, and namely I,
That wende and hadde a greet opinioun
That if I myghte escapen from prisoun,
Thanne hadde I been in joye and parfit heele,
That now I am exiled fro my wele.
Syn that I may nat seen you, Emelye,
I nam but deed, there nys no remedye.

UPON that oother syde, Palamon,
Whan that he wiste Arcite was agon,
Swich sorwe he maketh that the grete tour
Resouned of his youlyng and clamour;
The pure fettres on his shynes grete
Weren of his bittre, salte teeres wete.
Allas! quod he, Arcite, cosyn myn,
Of al our strif, God woot, the fruyt is thyn;
Thow walkest now in Thebes at thy large,
And of my wo yevest litel charge.
Thou mayest, syn thou hast wysdom & man hede,
Assemblen alle the folk of oure kynrede,
And make a werre so sharpe on this citee,
That by som aventure, or som tretee,
Thow mayest have hire to lady and to wyf
For whom that I mot nedes lese my lyf.
For as by wey of possibilitee,
Sith thou art at thy large, of prisoun free,
And art a lord, greet is thyn avauntage,
Moore than is myn that sterve here in a cage;
For I moot wepe and wayle whil I lyve,
With al the wo that prisoun may me yeve,
And eek with peyne that love me yeveth also,
That doubleth al my torment and my wo.
Therwith the fyr of jalousie up sterte
Withinne his brest, and hente him by the herte
So woodly, that he lyk was to biholde
The boxtree, or the asshen, dede and colde.
Thanne seyde he, O cruel goddes that governe
This world with byndyng of youre word eterne
And writen in the table of atthamaunt
Youre parlement and youre eterne graunt,
What is mankynde moore unto you holde
Than is the sheepe that rouketh in the folde?
For slayn is man, right as an oother beest,
And dwelleth eek in prison and arreest,
And hath siknesse and greet adversitee,
And ofte tymes giltelees pardee.
What governance is in this prescience,
That giltelees tormenteth innocence?
And yet encreseth this al my penaunce,
That man is bounden to his observaunce
For Goddes sake to letten of his wille,
Ther as a beest may all his lust fulfille;
And whan a beest is deed he hath no peyne,
But after his deeth man moot wepe and pleyne,
Though in this world he have care and wo,
Withouten doute may it stonden so.
The answer of this lete I to dyvynys,
But well I woot that in this world greet pyne ys.
Allas! I se a serpent or a theef,
That many a trewe man hath doon mescheef,

Goon at his large, and where hym list may turne;
But I moot been in prisoun thurgh Saturne,
And eek thurgh Juno, jalous and eek wood,
That hath destroyed wel ny al the blood
Of Thebes with his waste walles wyde;
And Venus sleeth me on that oother syde
For jalousie and fere of hym Arcite.

NOW wol I stynte of Palamon a lite,
And lete hym in his prisoun stille dwelle,
And of Arcite forth I wol yow telle.
The somer passeth, and the nyghtes longe
Encreessen double wise the peynes stronge
Bothe of the lovere and the prisoner.
I noot which hath the wofuller mester;
For shortly for to seyn, this Palamoun
Perpetuelly is dampned to prisoun
In cheynes and in fettres to been deed,
And Arcite is exiled upon his heed
For evere mo as out of that contree,
Ne nevere mo he shal his lady see.
Yow loveres, axe I now this questioun,
Who hath the worse, Arcite or Palamoun?
That oon may seen his lady day by day,
But in prisoun he moot dwellen alway;
That oother, wher hym list may ride or go,
But seen his lady shal he nevere mo.
Now demeth as yow liste, ye that han,
For I wol telle forth as I bigan.
Explicit pars prima. Sequitur pars secunda

WHAN that Arcite to The-
bes comen was,
Ful ofte a day he swelte
and seyde, Allas!
For seen his lady shal he
nevere mo.
And, shortly to conclud-
en al his wo,
So muche sorwe had
nevere creature
That is or shal, whil that the world may dure.
His slepe, his mete, his drynke, is hym biraft,
That lene he wexe and drye as is a shaft;
His eyen holwe, and grisly to biholde,
His hewe falow and pale as asshen colde,
And solitarie he was and evere allone,
And waillynge al the nyght, makynge his mone;
And if he herde song or instrument
Thanne wolde he wepe, he myghte nat be stent;
So feble eek were his spirits and so lowe,
And chaunged so that no man koude knowe
His speche nor his voys, though men it herde
And in his geere for al the world he ferde,
Nat oonly like the loveris maladye
Of Hereos, but rather lyk manye
Engendred of humour malencolik
Biforn his owene celle fantastik.
And shortly turned was al up so doun
Bothe habit and eek disposicioun
Of hym, this woful lovere daun Arcite.
WHAT sholde I al day of his wo endite?
Whan he endured hadde a yeer or two
This cruel torment and this peyne & woo,
At Thebes, in his contree, as I seyde,

13

A page from the Kelmscott *Chaucer*. $16\frac{3}{4}'' \times 11\frac{1}{4}''$.

He declared it to be 'the best-looking book issued since the seventeenth century', and added: 'I am so pleased with my book, typography, binding, and must I say it, literary matter, that I am any day to be seen huggling it up, and am become a spectacle to Gods and men because of it.' His enthusiasm rings true, but this was a passing fancy, for even then he was in hot pursuit of more opulent beauties.

It was the magnificence of the Kelmscott adventure which impressed and influenced printers, professional and amateur, and resuscitated the curious vogue for so-called 'Private Press' books artificially rarefied and deliberately beautified. But, in spite of many extravagances and some few absurdities, the Kelmscott influence has been beneficial. Morris reasserted sound principles, and the richness of his books helped to secure their acceptance. 'The road of excess leads to the palace of wisdom.' The style of the books themselves, because of their massive individuality, must always provoke differences of opinion, but in the

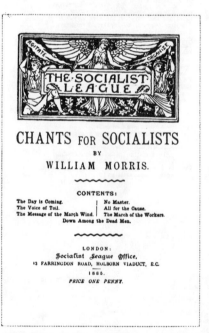

A typical Morris pamphlet. 7½″ × 5⅜″.

house of books there are many mansions, and room for all tastes, whims, and even fads.

I prefer my books pocketable, flexible, and legible. In the Kelmscott books these qualities are not sufficiently balanced. Each is there in some measure, but something is invariably added to weaken proportion. William Morris (or worse, Burne-Jones) is always getting between reader and author. I like my Chaucer neat. Morris produced Chaucer as Henry Irving and Beerbohm Tree produced Shakespeare. I suspect that enthusiasts for such productions are not readers. The idea is supported by the fact that the majority of Kelmscotts are still in mint state; it is not easy to meet a copy bearing the honourable and endearing scars of use.

Legibility is relative, as I am reminded by my own experience, for myself when young did eagerly frequent Pickering's *Diamond Classics*—a practice I should probably have defended with conviction based upon sight rather than insight. I take a different view to-day, not only of miniature types, but of rules and spacings generally. Morris granted the necessity of legibility. In this he differed from another poet and amateur of printing, Robert Bridges, who used Gothic characters for the Daniel Press edition of his poems to induce slow ingestion. Morris believed that solidity of type and setting made for easy reading. By solid type he meant 'without needless excrescences' or 'the thickening or thinning of the line', which, with reservations, can be defended. Density of type area is a different matter and, if I admit charm, I reserve the right to question even aesthetical

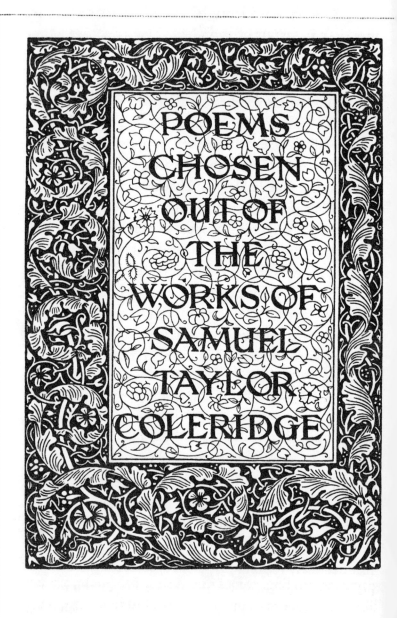

Title-page of the Kelmscott *Coleridge*. Designed by William Morris. 8¼″× :

propriety in favour of legibility. The solid page is impressive: solidity inspires confidence, but confidence, as we know, is often illusion and not always guiltless of trickery. The first edition of *The Roots of the Mountains* would probably have been more readable with than without rules.

But although legibility must always be the first rule of printing, there are other important principles. Morris summed them up in the word 'beauty' with impressive but dubious results, because of his predilection for ornamentation. Any plain space for him was an opportunity for decoration, or, in Ruskin's words, for 'the expression of man's joy in his work'. He would go out of his way to make books bigger than they need be so that he might have more space to fill with his and Burne-Jones's illustrations. His type-faces became picturesque, his margins inclined to pomposity, and his paper was pretentious. The Kelmscott books are overdressed. They ask you to look at them rather than to read them. You can't get away from their overwhelming typography, and, even if you could, you might still be cheated of your author by their high-minded purpose, for in addition to being the creations of an impressive genius the Kelmscott books were protests against the logical conclusions of mechanical book-production.

All these things are hindrances to reading, and I still believe that to be read is the destiny of a book, and that reading is best when you are least conscious of print or paper or binding. Since the Kelmscott books are not likely to induce that condition they must remain museum pieces, typographical monuments—beautiful and ineffectual angels beating in the void their luminous wings in vain.

II

WILLIAM CAXTON

WILLIAM CAXTON WAS ONE OF THOSE VERSATILE ENGLISH-men of the middle class to whom we owe much both in material and mental enterprise. Such men (Samuel Pepys was one of them, William Morris another) are adventurers in the true sense of a mishandled word. They are not always spectacular and do not necessarily wander far afield; sometimes indeed their activities are surprisingly limited in geographical range. They are of the order of stay-at-home adventurers who are content to discover continents in the cosmography of themselves. William Caxton, who was a successful and distinguished merchant adventurer in the woollen trade, did leave the Weald of Kent (where he was born about the year 1422) for London, and eventually journeyed abroad and lived for many years in the great textile centres of Holland, Flanders, and Brabant. He roamed as far away as Cologne, where he is supposed to have learnt printing, and it was in the 'holy cyte of Colen' that he had his first experience of the printing-press, but it was not until he returned home to Westminster that he entered fully upon his vocation as a printer, and did those things which have conferred immortality upon his name and made his printing-office at Westminster famous as the starting-place here in England of that book-culture which has done so much to inform, inspire, and shape the character of our civilization.

The art of printing from movable types would have

been introduced into England sooner or later, for the novel craft had captured the imagination of cultured and curious people in all those countries which were bubbling with the new wine of learning. Chance made Caxton the pioneer of printing in England; but it was a happy chance, for this business-man happened to combine astuteness in commerce and a keen love of learning with a courageous and unconventional respect for the vernacular. He may have lacked any serious knowledge of Latin, but being a man of means and individuality he had the courage to be himself and talk his own language. Whatever the cause, he was clearly aware of the fact that he was a reformer, and, indeed, was encouraged even in his earlier efforts by the thought that he was serving his country by translating a work not hitherto to be had 'in oure englissh langage'. Later he came to look upon the dissemination of literature by means of the new art of printing with the zeal of a missioner.

He was thus not only the pioneer of printing in England, though that would have been sufficient to establish his memory. William Caxton was an amateur of letters and a bookman, loving Chaucer the modern writer, no less than Virgil and the Classics. By his translations he helped to lay the foundations of literary English and by his publications to take the first step towards popular acceptance of books for, like his modern follower, William Morris, he delighted in printing those books which most appealed to his personal taste as a reader; and, in addition, he liked to think that his publications might be beneficial to the minds or morals of his fellow countrymen. He was in fact a familiar English type, one of those who enjoy their own whims better if they can persuade themselves that by following them they are improving the minds or manners of others, or, at least, keeping themselves out of mischief. He admits as much in the preface to *The Recuyell of the Historyes of Troye*, which he translated out of the French. Here, he explains, since every man is bound by the counsel of wise men 'to eschewe slothe and ydlenes whyche is moder and nourysshar of vyces', and having 'no grete charge or ocupacion' he puts himself into the 'vertuous ocupacion and besynesse' of translating these 'strange and meruaylous historyes' from 'the fayr langage of frenshe' into that of 'the royame of englond'.

Caxton was, however, neither an eccentric person nor even an intellectual. He was a normal business man, but of more than average intelligence. The sort of man, one would imagine, for we have few personal details, who first establishes himself on an economic basis and then enjoys a hobby. In his case the tail ultimately wagged the dog, for William Caxton the successful mercer became William Caxton the printer, and probably came to live by the thing he lived for. If he started his press at Westminster as a hobby, it certainly ended as a whole-time job. It is evident also that he paid little or no attention in the early stages of his enterprise to the aesthetics of the new craft.

The probable explanation of this apparent carelessness is that he felt, unconsciously no doubt, that unaffected printing best suited plain language. He was probably interested in becoming a plain and practical printer rather than a stylish printer, hoping, perchance, that his vernacular books would look their part and not ape the aristocratic manners of the then fashionable Latin classics, Bibles, and liturgical books. No doubt he could have followed good examples had he wished, for unlike many new mechanical crafts in our own time, such as the building of aeroplanes, automobiles, radio sets, and gramophones, there was no excuse for a prolonged archaic period. The early printer frankly imitated the familiar medieval manuscript, and the transition from one to the other was easy because it did not involve the entire abandonment of handicraft for machine-craft. The conditions imposed were the more amenable substitution of one kind of handicraft for another. Printing did not become entirely mechanical until within living memory. To be sure there are considerable differences between the operations of scribe and printer, but a comparison of written and printed books reveals as much room for the expression of a traditional or even a personal sense of design in one as the other, and a further examination over a long period proves that printed books as a whole, in so far as the letterpress is concerned, are less standardized than manuscripts, and not less beautiful.

It is not surprising, therefore, to find that Gutenberg's Bible is a typographical masterpiece, and that many of the lesser incunabula are well designed and satisfying examples of the craft of printing. It is all the more puzzling to find such artlessness in the productions of the first English printer, and whatever the cause, carelessness,

haste, indifference, or a preference for a relatively informal typography based upon the vernacular romances
in manuscript which were not as formal in their calligraphy as a Latin codex, it is clear that, whilst grasping
the importance of movable types, he failed to realize
their full aesthetic significance. He was, at first at all
events, a business man rather than a craftsman—and
perhaps that not unfamiliar phenomenon, a business
man in a hurry. It has been suggested, and not without
justice, that his typographical style did not improve until
he was threatened with competition, and that even then
the improvement was largely due to the influence of a
new foreman, Wynken de Worde, who ultimately
became his successor.

There is some evidence for this assumption, for it is
clear from Caxton's own statements that his enterprise
at its inception was inspired by a desire to disseminate
literature in English. He may have been a merchant first
and last, but he was also an amateur of literature devoted
to poetry and history; and the fact that he published
volumes of wise sayings might reasonably be thought
to indicate that he possessed the average busy man's
liking for wisdom in tabloid form. Further, and this
must never be overlooked, he was a public-spirited man
playing a part in the general affairs of his trade as livery-
man, guildmaster, and Governor of the English Nation
at Bruges. It was natural, therefore, that such a man
should come to look upon printing as a new means of
distributing knowledge and extending the delights of
reading, especially if they could be linked up with the

development of his native tongue, the love of which was doubtless enhanced by the inevitable nostalgia produced in one who, though he spoke French like a native because he had lived for 'the space of xxx yere for the most parte in the centres of Braband', was born in Kent where, he doubts not, 'is spoken as brode and rude Englissh as in ony place in englond'. This rude English he always loved, and when opportunity came he sought to give it a common form and make it more accessible to his countrymen. But there is less evidence that he arrived at this notion in advance of his knowledge of printing than that it came to him as he familiarized himself with the mysteries and possibilities of the new craft.

In his reading he had come upon and enjoyed *Le Recueil des Histoires de Troyes* by Raoul le Fevre. It was what we should call a best-seller, and he had tried his hand at translating some of it into English. At that time, like the author of the book, he was in the service of the House of Burgundy, and it was 'at the commandement of the right hye myghty and vertuose Pryncesse hys redoubtyd lady, Margaret by the grace of God, Duchesse of Bourgoyne', who had read and enjoyed his manuscript, that he undertook to 'make an ende of the resydue then not translated'. He began the task at Bruges, in 1468, when he was in his forty-seventh year, continued it at Ghent, and completed the work in about two years and a half at Cologne.

The Duchess of Burgundy was pleased with the manuscript copy which Caxton gave her, and her expressed appreciation made the translation popular. The demand for copies increased so rapidly that, in self-defence, Caxton turned to the printing-press as a means of escape from the drudgery of writing copies for his friends, for, he tells us, his hand was weary, his pen worn, his 'eyen dimmed with overmoche lokyng on the whit paper', and furthermore, his courage 'not so prone and redy to laboure' as of yore, for 'age crepeth on me dayly and febleth all the bodye'. It was thus in order to accelerate the circulation of his own translations that he decided to practise the new craft at Bruges, where he was a man of substance and head of a considerable English colony.

Printing, for Caxton, was thus at first a time-saving device. It soon, however, revealed itself to him as a means of spreading knowledge and literature in a co-ordinated English, and in that intention and pursuit he has put us more in his debt than if he had been merely the pioneer of a craft which eventually would have been introduced into England just as it was being introduced into other countries. It was our good fortune that printing was brought to Westminster by a man of such intelligence that he became the pioneer of a standard English in an age of pedants inclined to view the vernacular with so much indifference that each county almost was left to its own linguistic devices.

William Caxton's contribution to typography, however, is not memorable solely because of its literary purpose and reputation. His work as a printer pure and simple did progress, and on more than one occasion he altered the character of his type-faces, until at his best period his typography achieves a distinction of its own as well as the kind of charm possessed by all honest craftsmanship, no matter how crude, and especially of craftsmanship in its nonage.

It is not surprising that the books produced by such a man and under such circumstances should occupy, with the first editions of the works of Shakespeare, the predominant place in English bibliography; and, if we know almost as little of William Caxton as we do of William Shakespeare, the devotion of such Caxtonians as William Blades, Henry Bradshaw, Gordon Duff, A. W. Pollard, and Seymour de Ricci has made his works, their status and characteristics, familiar to all bibliophiles.

His prentice work was completed at Bruges, where he printed three books, one of them his own translation of Jehan de Vignay's version of Jacobus de Cessolis's *The game and playe of the chesse*, which was finished in 1475. In the following year he set up house in the Almonry at Westminster Abbey, and a few weeks later the first piece of English printing was born. It took the form of an *Indulgence* issued by the Abbot of Abingdon to Henry Langly and his wife, Katherine, on December 13th, 1476. Until the discovery of this unique sheet in 1928, it was always assumed that *The Dictes or Sayenges of the phylosophers*, translated from the French of Guillaume de Tignonville by Earl Rivers (finished November 18th, 1477) was the earliest example of Caxton's printing. This work now takes second place, although it is still believed to be the first book printed in England.

One hundred books in all were made and published by Caxton, ninety-seven of them at Westminster. His literary taste was catholic and covered many subjects: games, morals, religion, poetry, and history. Indeed his 'list' though small would earn the respect of any modern publisher both for its variety and its quality. In addition to the books there were a number of indulgences and other documents which prove that Caxton was not only our first printer-publisher but also our first jobbing printer.

Eight different type-faces were used, all, after the manner of those cradle-days of typography, following closely the Gothic lettering. There is diversity both in the style and the quality of the early work, and, at the same time, marked progress towards conventional ripeness, which increased with the development of a more exact typographical technique. The type used for the *Recuyell* (1475) is obviously inferior to that used for the *Godfrey of Boloyne* (1481), yet it has a primitive charm, in spite of a certain clumsiness, which again seems to blend with the naïvety of an occasional irregularity in the outer edge of the type area, a defect which Caxton did not correct until 1480.

The extent and variety of this product both as regards works and typography prove that Caxton was a man of energy and resource. His range of types alone is an achievement. But more than that, more than his inventiveness and enterprise, must be reckoned the bookish foresight and intelligence of this pioneer of a new craft. Whatever faults his typography possessed were outweighed by that honesty of purpose by means of which he opened the way to the building of a great common language for his fellow countrymen. The very fact that he was a man of sound sense and general intelligence rather than a highly specialized scholar helped him in his task and assured his success. He himself had no illusions on that point, and more than once confessed that he was 'not lerned ne knowynge the arte of rethoryk ne of suche gaye termes as now be sayd in these dayes and used'. His aim was to be 'understonden of the redars and herers' for, he said, 'that shall suffyse'. It not only sufficed then but it is an example which every defender of the English language, whose foundations were so well and truly laid by William Caxton, follows to this day. And for that reason, if for no other, every bibliophile reveres his name and would rejoice in the possession of the smallest fragment of his printed work.

1933

III

CLAUD LOVAT FRASER: ILLUSTRATOR

THERE IS NO SURER WAY OF MISUNDERSTANDING THE CON-
tribution of Claud Lovat Fraser to contemporary art than
to attempt to docket him or to pigeon-hole his work. He
belonged to no category, ancient or modern. His work
has, of course, its origins and affinities. Spontaneous
artistic creation is so rare as to be almost unknown. Thus
Fraser, like greater and lesser artists, came under the
influence of painters and illustrators, both living and
dead—dead, as we shall see, in more senses than one. But
his following of others was never so absorbed as to lead
him into the cul-de-sac of archaism or the intricacies and
poses of modernism. He could be old-fashioned without
being archaic, just as he was modern without being
modernist. The style was most obviously the man; and
the style came early, crudely at first, but it had always
an inexplicable but instantly knowable quality. It then
set out to meet and be strengthened by association with
its kind, and ultimately returned to itself sound and
certain of aim, so that any one who saw his work would
recognize it as his. It is the fortune of very few who paint
or draw, or who try to paint or draw, to reach that distinction of style which separates without divorcing the
work from the opportunity of common appreciation.

He had an irrepressible love of drawing. From early
youth onwards he lived with pens and pencils, coloured
inks, and later, with water colours and, sometimes, oils.
It would be difficult to exaggerate the prodigality of his

genius. In a very literal sense he was drawing or awaiting an opportunity to draw during all his waking hours. He drew at meals, concerts, plays, lectures, during conversation, in church, in the trenches and camps during the War, and in or on any vehicle which might have been transporting him from one place to another. He would stop in a busy London street, pull out a sketch-book, or, failing that, an odd scrap of paper, to illustrate some conversational point with a humorous little drawing, or to make a note of something that had caught his quick eye among passers-by or in the general scene. He drew anything and everything out of an abundant creative energy, and from joy of observation. It was a kind of inspired scribbling, often childlike and incoherent, and not seldom crude and careless, especially in his early period, but his sketches were always individual and, at best, distinct in craftsmanship and observation. His prodigality has been revealed posthumously by the publication of several illustrated books retrieved from the mass of drawings and paintings of all kinds which he left behind him; and, apart even from this collection, the sketches in letters and on postcards and every imaginable scrap of paper scattered among his friends must be incalculable. A piece of paper rarely left his hands without bearing some mark of his zeal as an illustrator.

Although he extended his art in other directions—the theatre, pattern designing, advertisement decoration—and would, had he lived, have gone farther afield still, he never lost his earliest interest or relinquished his earliest practice of illustration. Even when he came to illustrate books which publishers were willing to print, he did not abandon the pleasant habit of making pictorial remarks, for that is what his illustrations were, about life as it passed by at all times on any oddment of paper that came readiest to his tireless and expressive hand. This passion for graphic comment is the key to his work as an illustrator: it explains the Lovat Fraser books and their curious isolation from most of the decorated books of his time. They have no connexion with any contemporary 'movement' or 'tendency'. Fraser laughed at movements; and reformers, whether in art (particularly in art) or in other directions, were for him objects of satire. Nothing, for instance, could be more marked than the difference between his books and those of such conscious beautifiers as William Morris, Walter Crane, Charles Ricketts, and Lucien Pissarro. The essence of the Lovat Fraser books is that their design is absence of design, their charm integral rather than applied. Impressionists would probably have called him a 'literary' draughtsman, especially if they had known, as his friends knew, how much he loved and depended upon books and literary impressions in his early days. They would have been wrong. At the same time it would not be right to ignore this literary source of inspiration which made him, in spite of his youth, one of the best read of living artists, and one who succeeded in translating reading into drawing, as another kind of reader might have made marginal notes.

His decorations of books, like the sketches in his personal correspondence, were thus pictorial comments. They have the appearance of being ornamental or decorative by accident. The parallel is between, say, the deliberate decoration of the wall of a room with patterned paper or frieze or dado, and the placing in an undecorated room of a choice piece of pottery, a little statue, or an occasional picture unobtrusively framed. Lovat Fraser's method as an illustrator of books coincides with the latter—he ornamented rather than decorated. This is in keeping with the man. He was a *poseur*, but an agreeable one. Some of those who did not know him well were irritated by his mannered wit and his dandified bearing. But to most it was a refreshment, because it was always good-humoured. His remarks about life, art, and persons were frequent but not flowing: vignettes and cameos, not tapestries; their very essence was a modish detachment following a pause and succeeded by a little gasp of amusement at his own humour or audacity. His illustrations have this variability, this intermittence, and the pose which is inseparable from a deliberate comment or a studied remark. They lack everything in the nature of repetition. They are formal in a curiously informal way; natural as a park or garden is natural; conventional, but the convention is their own.

He was born into an atmosphere of art, for his mother was an accomplished amateur painter, but he went his own way; and, save for a few months in the studio of Richard Sickert, he escaped the art schools and the studios. He was a self-made artist, and evolved his style out of the prints and drawings which pleased him best. The influences under which he came were few and definite. But perhaps it would be more exact to call them preferences, for he did not follow them so much as find himself in them. His earliest enthusiasms were for the crude and quaint cuts of the old chapbooks and broadsides, and he sought out their correlatives in contemporary arts as well as in the more consciously 'quaint' work of the immediate past. His elation on the discovery of Alfred Crowquill's *Impresses Quaint*, somewhere about 1910, was tremendous; and he revelled in Charles Hindley's *Life and Times of James Catnach* (1878) and *The History of the Catnach Press* (1887). In these two volumes the investigator may find the origins of the types, covers, and 'lay-outs' of the *Flying Fame* publications. He made a collection of chapbooks and broadsides, and hoarded with reverent care any drawings of Rowlandson which came within his purchasing power. He also liked to accumulate coloured military and fashion plates of the eighteenth and early nineteenth centuries. The more impossible military gear, vast shakos, tailed and tight-waisted tunics in vivid reds, blues, greens, and pipe-clayed facings, long trailing swords, and extravagant fashions, periwigs, capacious stocks and strapped pantaloons, fascinated him and helped to form his art.

Among his contemporaries he was attracted to the work of Jack B. Yeats, whose little books about pirates, and broadsides about highwaymen, ballad-mongers, brigands, and other wayfaring folks, then being issued from the Dun Emer Press at Dundrum, Dublin, played an important part among these early influences. It was natural also that he should be moved by the work of Gordon Craig: first by the charming and very personal drawings which Craig dropped about the typography of too few books, and ultimately extended to the periodical pages of *The Mask*, and later by Gordon Craig's creations in the art of the theatre itself, which was Fraser's last adventure.

Finally, his always lively appreciation of caricature must not be overlooked. Apart from his gifts as an illustrator, he had a genius for satire. He admired the work of Ospovat and Max Beerbohm; watched with a critical eye the pages of *Jugend* and *L'Assiette au Beurre*, but succeeded in laughing without being contaminated by those violent continental efforts in the art of satirical bludgeoning. He escaped also the baneful influence of Aubrey Beardsley: 'stale incense, *n'est-ce pas?*' was how he summed up that genius of the decadence. The other 'movements' left him equally unmoved. We were once looking together at an early Picasso—'reminds me of a tramway ticket of genius', he remarked.

His first book was characteristic of his then predominant enthusiasm, but bears small relation to the kind of illustrated book with which his name was later associated. It is the now almost inaccessible, tall, narrow volume in grey boards and linen back, called *Six Caricatures: By Lovat C. Fraser*, and was issued in an edition of twenty-five copies in January 1910, for friends who paid him a few shillings a copy to defray part of the cost of manufacture. The notabilities caricatured are Charles Wyndham, Martin Harvey, Oscar Asche, Lord Roberts, Keir Hardie, and Israel Zangwill. The drawings are printed in black from zinco blocks and coloured by hand. They are obviously prentice work, showing the influence of Ospovat with that artist's fiercer satire muted to a more playful humour. Almost immediately afterwards he did better work in caricature, including the masterly study of Lord Alverstone and cheerfully clever caricatures of the much-caricatured Hall Caine, Bernard Shaw, G. K. Chesterton, and, finally and most amusingly, himself as a massive dandy of a composite type—say George IV– D'Orsay–Whistler.

One of the earliest and most pronounced enjoyments of these early days was the little adventure which produced the *Flying Fame* chapbooks and broadsides. It was a game—almost a chance game. The idea was the outcome of much playful talk, banter, and sketching and squib-writing by a group of writers and a painter or so who used to meet for coffee in the smoking-room of a Strand teashop during 1912. Towards the end of that year three members of the group—Lovat Fraser, Ralph Hodgson, and the writer—decided to pool the sum of five pounds each plus certain pieces of poetry and prose for the purpose of producing a few little books and sheets of verse, in the manner of the old chapbooks and broadsides. They were to be designed and illustrated by Fraser. The name of the venture, *Flying Fame*, was suggested by Ralph Hodgson, and he also ensured the success of the scheme by allowing us to reprint from the *Saturday Review*, where they lay buried, several of his finest poems (then scarcely known), and these were augmented by contributions from Walter de la Mare and James Stephens. I supplied a prose piece, acted as publicist, and helped in typographical matters. Lovat Fraser invented or adapted the formats after Catnach, made the decorations and lay-outs, hunted for and chose the quaint types and cover papers, wrote verses, coloured the early issues of the hand-coloured ones, and in fact lived and worked for the job, night and day, until the little publications won for themselves a deserved reputation among people who like such things for themselves and not because they ought to like them or because other people like them or because they may go up in value. The life of the 'Press' was arrested, like so many other good things, by the War, and never revived. *Flying Fame* publications are now among the more desirable bibelots of the book collectors.

The chief publications of the *Flying Fame* Press are *Eve and other Poems; The Bull; The Song of Honour* and *The Mystery and other Poems*, by Ralph Hodgson; *Five New Poems*, by James Stephens; *The Two Wizards and other Songs*, and *Six Essays in the Eighteenth Century*, by Richard Honeywood (i.e. Claud Lovat Fraser), and *Town: An Essay*, by Holbrook Jackson. There were large-paper editions of most of them, and a few copies on imitation vellum with covers printed in gold; these and some of the smaller paper copies were coloured by hand by the artist himself. The typography was deliberately crude, and so were the drawings which were dotted about the pages, generally at top and bottom. But the effect is pleasing as well as quaint, showing what can be done when good taste operates with even crude type faces. Many of the drawings are trivial, but some are

No. 1

EVE

AND

Other Poems.

By *RALPH HODGSON.*

—

PRICE SIXPENCE.

Eve, first edition, issued in yellow wrappers, printed in black. $6\frac{1}{2}'' \times 4\frac{1}{8}''$.

among the best of Lovat Fraser's work, and all possess the grace and charm of a very young but very real genius. In 1914 he published *Pirates*, a quarto reprint of a 1735 chapbook. He illustrated the volume with full-page drawings of distinguished pirates on coloured papers and a number of cuts of ships and seamen.

Lovat Fraser's next phase as an illustrator was conditioned entirely by the War. He was in training soon after the outbreak of hostilities. In 1915 he was in the trenches before Ypres, and in action at Loos and elsewhere on that perilous front. During those months and onwards, until he returned to home service with shattered nerves, his pencil was rarely idle. The post carried to his friends innumerable letters and sketches of military life and war scenes, vigorously assembled lines depicting swiftly and with the vividness of genius aspects of the War from a peculiarly Fraserian point of view. One of the most beautiful of the drawings of this period is a masterly study of the battered Cloth Hall of Ypres, the original sketch of which was drawn in the trenches under fire, but the majority of them represent various types of soldiers— British, Belgian, and French officers and men, and German prisoners. Few of these sketches have been published.

In 1916 he strove successfully to recapture his connexion with the world of books. The first efforts were a couple of diminutive pamphlets: *The Fairies' Farewell*, by Richard Corbet; the *Three Poems* by Kenneth Hare. These trifles were printed by A. T. Stephens of St. Martin's Lane, who was responsible for the composition of the *Flying Fame* chapbooks, and they were sold at sixpence each by Everard Meynell at his Serendipity Bookshop in Museum Street. The covers are crudely but richly decorated in black and white, and there are two or three typical Fraser cuts with the text. That year also Harold Monro published, at the Poetry Bookshop, *Nurse Lovechild's Legacy*—'a mighty fine collection of the most noble, and memorable and veracious Nursery Rhymes, now first embellished by C. L. F.' The cover and title-page have a deliberately crude arabesque border, but the numerous thumbnail cuts scattered about the text represent Fraser at his best as a chapbook illustrator. These little drawings, vivacious, humorous, and original, would make any illustrator unforgettable.

His interests were now moving towards the theatre and to larger pictures. But he continued to fill his odd moments and reams of old paper, retrieved from forgotten and half-filled scrapbooks of a century or so ago, with his amazing little sketches; and he planned many books, some of which have since been published. His style was becoming more deliberate and more careful, his drawing more certain, yet he lost little of his early naïvety. The two most notable of the books of this period are *The Lute of Love*, a collection of his favourite poems of the sixteenth and seventeenth centuries, with cuts fore and aft of each poem and a well composed title-page, and *Helicon Hill*: 'a pleasant posy of rather wild flowers gathered on the foot-hills of Parnassus, and judged very meet for the brows of contemporary rhymers, by Felix Folio, Gent., of London'. These volumes were issued by

TOWN.

SINCE it is man's privilege, and, I hope, delight, to sanctify that which he likes by praise, let me, liker of many things, sanctify in such time-hallowed manner that which upon most days in most years, I like above all places.

Let me praise Town.

If you tell me it is unnecessary, I shall agree with you, for has not mankind, from the days when he was a wild thing, perpetually cast halo upon halo upon the brows of his favorite? Nevertheless, it is rarely too late to praise what is good, especially when there exist those

5

Title-page of *Nurse Lovechild's Legacy.* 5⅜″ × 3¼″.

First page of the *Flying Fame* chapbook, *Town.* 6⅛″ × 4⅛″.

THIS COLLECTION HAS BEEN COMPILED FROM XVIIIth AND EARLY SIXTH CENTURY CHAPBOOKS

Decorations by C. Lovat Fraser

The Château May Jacques built

CONTENTS.

Nurse Lovechild's Legacy, frontispiece and contents. 5⅜″ × 3¼″.

Selwyn & Blount. An equally notable volume is the *Nursery Rhymes*, issued in quarto by T. C. & E. C. Jack, with brilliant pictures in colour, bolder, richer, and more mature than any of his earlier bookwork, and many of the familiar little cuts in black and white.

Among the posthumous colour books more recently issued are *The Woodcutter's Dog*, by Charles Nodier, and *The Luck of the Bean-Rows*. A further advance in style is shown here, higher finish without loss of vigour or the sense of fun which characterized most of his illustrations. They were published by Daniel O'Connor. *A Selection of the Poems of Charles Cotton* (The Poetry Bookshop) and, more recently, *The House of Vanities*, by Hayter Preston (John Lane), are decorated in the earlier chapbook manner, but the former has a bold conventionalized floral border of mature design. The fine edition of *The Beggar's Opera*, published in 1921, with its reproductions of some of the drawings made for the costumes of the play and a few cuts, is less characteristic of the artist as represented in all the earlier books. It was the last book to be prepared by himself for press, but he did not live to see it published. The volume has a dignity and even a charm, but it would seem to indicate a definite change in taste, greater reserve, more austerity: in short, Claud Lovat Fraser at length grown up.

Few illustrators have shown so much versatility within so limited a range as Lovat Fraser. It is idle to predict what he might have done had he lived longer,[1] and ungenerous to his very real achievement to lay stress on

1 Claud Lovat Fraser died at the age of 31 in 1921.

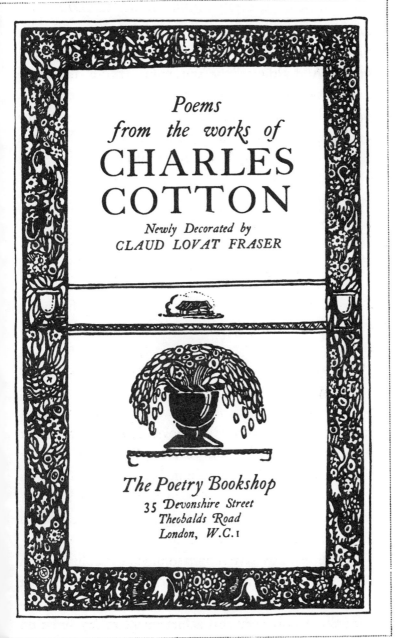

Poems
from the works of
CHARLES
COTTON
Newly Decorated by
CLAUD LOVAT FRASER

The Poetry Bookshop
35 *Devonshire Street*
Theobalds Road
London, W.C.1

Title-page of Charles Cotton's *Poems*, designed by Claud Lovat Fraser. 8½″ × 5½″.

what might have been. He gave us an abundance of pictorial comment full of high spirits, ingenuity, and grace. And although he sometimes ignores the more severe conventions of book decoration, he never denies or defies his early bookish origins. Lovat Fraser's 'impresses quaint' rest on the page like flowers, as though at a magic touch the book had burst into bloom.

1923

IV

LOVAT FRASER'S DESIGNS FOR
'A SHROPSHIRE LAD'[1]

WHEN THE CRITICS HAVE SAID THEIR SAY AND TIME HAS winnowed from the work of Claud Lovat Fraser all personal and contemporary associations, his book decorations and those unattached pictures which approximate to them will be remembered as his most original and most permanent contribution to art. Albert Rutherston has expressed the opinion that Lovat Fraser 'never surpassed in delicate inventiveness or richness of imaginative quality those decorations done for the early chapbooks and broadsides which were published under the title *Flying Fame*'. As a matter of fact, and it is important if a correct appreciation of Lovat Fraser's work is desired, he never passed out of what may be called his chapbook period, because that period was the man. He may have wandered in other directions, as, for instance, into the theatre, where he achieved notable successes, but such wanderings were excursions. There is, of course, room in an artist's life for many inventions and adventures, even when that life is short, but in the greater number of instances those inventions and adventures crystallize about a central theme or trick or whim which contains and expresses the man and forms his art. Claud Lovat Fraser, brief as his days were, had several periods, but the chapbook period survived them all—even his

---

1 Introduction to *Sixty-three Unpublished Designs by Claud Lovat Fraser*. (The First Edition Club, 1924).

invasion of the stage was through the door of a toy-theatre

For that reason alone the discovery and publication of any of the work of this period which has not hitherto been accessible is desirable; and, where the drawings represent a carefully conceived scheme of decoration for one of the most distinguished poetical works of our time, the matter is of first-rate importance. Decorations were made for A. E. Housman's lyric-sequence, *A Shropshire Lad*. Housman would not, however, permit them to be printed with his poems. That is a matter which need not detain us long, and the writer should certainly be the final arbiter. At the same time, the refusal of a set of Lovat Fraser's decorations is not likely to escape comment and perhaps censure.

It may once again reopen the pleasant and eternally recurrent discussion of the rights and wrongs of illustrating literature in general; and, since people will argue about books, that is as good a basis as any other and capable of provoking a variety of opinions. It is not my intention here or elsewhere to enter the lists on either, or indeed any side, for there are many more than two, and I am upheld in my decision by a deep-rooted prejudice against the decoration of books or other things, still more against illustrations unless they are inevitable and indispensable interpretations of the text. And since above all essences I prefer my poetry neat, I would, were I inclined to dogmatize, lay it down as an axiom that poetry should never be illustrated and hardly ever decorated, and even then almost imperceptibly. Which argument may be suitably pointed by a familiar story from the legend of Mr. Whistler. The artist, so it is said, was once asked why he did not paint the Doge's Palace, or some other of the more 'popular' buildings of Venice. He replied, 'Sir' (or Madam, as the case may be, and I rather fancy it was Madam), 'the Doge's Palace is a work of art already!' So is poetry. I only wish Housman agreed with me. That he did not is evident because he permitted *A Shropshire Lad* to appear in an illustrated edition. I am consoled, however, by the thought that these drawings can only be kept apart from the great verse which inspired them for duration of the copyright. Twenty or thirty years hence publishers will be falling over one another in an effort to have first honours (and profits) from bringing about their wedding.

All of which is a little wide of the mark, for apart from any relationship to the poems which these drawings are supposed to illustrate, and which, in fact, they do illustrate, they possess independent value as examples of Lovat Fraser's most characteristic work at its most mature stage. As illustrations of *A Shropshire Lad*, and even a decoration must have an illustrative genesis, they have not the inevitability of the earlier chapbook work or that of the thumbnail sketches of *Nurse Lovechild's Legacy*, perhaps the most inspired and appropriate of his works at the time. But what of that? They were called up by the book and they are a legitimate, if individually imagined, comment upon it. They are *A Shropshire Lad* apropos of Lovat Fraser, and, as such, have interest and value. Being of Salopian descent myself and

Specimen drawings made by Claud Lovat Fraser for *A Shropshire Lad*.

familiar with the Shropshire scene, I should cavil at some of his landscapes. They are certainly not Salopian as I recall the scenario of that proud shire. They smack rather of Hertfordshire, where the artist spent so many happy days. But that is no more than cavil, for the Shropshire Lad's country might have been anywhere south of the Mersey and the Humber, just as Hardy's Wessex might have stretched northwards to include Mercia, and eastwards to include Sussex. The scenario of both poems and pictures is the English countryside, and that should be enough. *A Shropshire Lad* must stand or fall by its poetry, not its local colour.

Another fault, and this perhaps is a little more serious, is a tendency towards a theatrical interpretation of certain themes. That is not excusable in the treatment of such poems. Instances are the wholly inappropriate stage peasants and the inadequate and obviously stuffed Mithridates, to illustrate the humorous-grotesquerie of the famous penultimate poem, the veiled wisdom of which Fraser seems to have missed. On the other hand, there is much to be said for the point of view of such drawings as v, ix, xv, xvi, xxiii, and xlvii;[1] and the purely ornamental pieces are always admirable, because they are at once non-committal and Lovat Fraser. One could easily imagine more appropriate, but no more individual, decorations for these poems. The artist certainly does not show here the inevitable flair for his subject which was so evident in his earlier work in this *genre*. I suspect that his appreciation of the poems was born of respect

1 The numbers refer to the volume containing the drawings.

rather than affection. Such a conclusion would be in character.

The decorations as drawings have an independent interest. I have described them as mature, but they represent many stages of this side of Lovat Fraser's work. Here and there is the happy spontaneity of the nursery rhyme days of frank play, but more often they reveal a responsibility, a consciousness of design, indicating, perhaps, the conventionalization of a happy gift.

1924

V

THE DOUBLE CROWN CLUB: EARLY HISTORY[1]

THE GENESIS OF THE CLUB IS ALREADY OBSCURE, THAT IS, if we seek a first cause, for, like all historical origins, first causes as distinct from precipitating causes are a matter of opinion. Whistler believed that art happened, and so, among other pleasant things, did the Double Crown Club. The analogy may be extended according to taste. But art could not happen unless the times were propitious, and away back in the early 1920's there was a predisposition for such a club among the then scattered members who were rescuing typography from the effects of the medievalism of William Morris and the sentimentalisms of L'Art Nouveau.

Before the Club was formed there had been flutterings in the world of printing, so in order to realize our significance we must picture a period of typographical complacency ruffled by the shrapnel of a small self-confident group of disturbers of the peace, who called themselves typographers. Some of them were printers as well, but printing experience was not then believed to be necessary to salvation. A typographer (new style) did not print, he designed printing. There were some stiff-necked traditionalists, and probably there are some still, who objected to this division of labour, but it would seem that results have justified the departure from rectitude.

1 A paper read at the 50th Dinner of the Double Crown Club at the Café Royal, October 9th, 1935.

The typographer stood towards the printing office as the producer of plays to the playhouse, and at that time he was frankly experimental. He knew what he wanted, but he was not yet certain how to get it. His enemies were the satisfied commercial printers and the amateurs of 'fine printing'. The one, in the main, looked upon the machine as a means of increasing production and profits without undue insistence upon taste; the other looked upon mechanical printing as the monster which had destroyed taste by supplanting the tradition of handicraft. The new men had no quarrel with machines or traditions but they refused to be bullied by either of them. Perhaps they had a greater regard for the past than those traditionalists who believed that good printing stopped short at the cultivated court of King Edward V. The typographers of the 1920's believed that good printing was possible at all times and for all purposes, and they believed that design and craftsmanship were not inconsistent with mechanical production whether the object were a book, a folder, or a label. Such ideas may seem trite enough to-day, but at that time they were revolutionary, and the young men who propagated them were probably put into the category of firebrands.

Their activities were not confined to the Metropolis. There were sporadic outbreaks in the suburbs and the provinces. Walter Lewis was striving valiantly at Norwood to save the Ballantyne tradition. Harold Curwen at Plaistow went modern at a tender age. Fred Phillips, supported by Herrick, was breeding Wembley lions in a den of Daniels at Brixton. Farther afield the rumblings could be heard. Eric Gill (then A. E. R. Gill) was laying his prentice hands on toy-books at Ditchling. Bernard Newdigate was 'warbling his native wood notes wild' at Stratford-on-Avon. Not far away Herbert Simon was astonishing the midlands at Witton, and away in the north William Maxwell was resisting the temptations of 'fine printing' at Edinburgh.

But the real revolution was hottest in Manchester. What Lancashire says to-day England will say to-morrow. And it did. C. W. Hobson was throwing silhouettes into space and harmonizing type, illustrations, and copy, in an entirely new design for advertisement. Grimmond was already in charge of the Hobson studio, where Haslam Mills was doing copy, specimens of which may be included in a future *Oxford* (or Cambridge) *Book of English Prose*. Later this new force was augmented by Walter Lewis and Stanley Morison who directed the Hobsonian attack from the cloisters at Heaton Mersey.

At this time Oxford and Cambridge were still dreaming among their spires and their dreams were perhaps a little troubled. It seemed that each of them felt that something ought to be done about it. But momentous decisions were pending. And with the arrival of John Johnson at Oxford and Walter Lewis at Cambridge the immemorial, typographically speaking, again became memorable.

London did not fail to sit up and take notice. Before the War Gerard Meynell, with the portcullis of Westminster on his shield, had been brandishing his sword in

the *Imprint*, and in his own printing office; Joseph
Thorp was challenging contemporary complacency in
both printing and lettering from the W. H. S. re-
doubt at Southwark; and Percy Smith was inviting
young printers to 'say it with flowers' at Clerkenwell.
Later Oliver Simon was detailed by Harold Curwen to
spread the light from Bloomsbury, and at about the
same time Francis Meynell swam into our ken, flash-
ing an astonishing versatility at first daintily, almost
shyly, from Romney Street, later more boldly from
the sign of the Pelican in Tudor Street, and ever
since he has kept the typographically minded on tip-
toe of expectation from Great James Street over against
Gray's Inn.

The diversions of typographers and printers were supported by members of allied crafts and trades. Illustrators and publishers linked up. Artists did commercial
work without losing their integrity as artists. Claud
Lovat Fraser with his Regency mind and Twentieth
Century technique did any job of work that came to his
hand, from trade circulars and booklets to *éditions de
luxe* and stage *décors*. McKnight Kauffer's mechanistic
emblems began to crackle in advertisements, and to
explode on the hoardings. Paul Nash made a brief excursion into typography, bringing a new abstraction to the
decoration of books; Albert Rutherston made form and
colour dance to a new measure that was refreshingly old;
and Thomas Lowinsky wedded a modern ornamentation
to the printed page. All these efforts began to have an
effect upon publishing. Established publishers were at

first fitful and hesitant, admitting into their lists an odd book here and there which had been designed, the rest being left to the 'comps'. Young publishers with no bad traditions to live down readily adapted themselves to the new typographical conditions: notably Jonathan Cape under G. Wren Howard. Constable was awakened typographically by Michael Sadleir, and there is at least one instance of an elder publisher taking the modern path of the designed book: Chatto & Windus under the guidance of C. H. C. Prentice.

Leaders of the movement occasionally sought out their kind, and in 1922 there was an attempt at co-ordination of effort in the form of a publishing house which should produce works of accredited authors, past and present, in formats designed according to the unwritten laws of the new typography. The members of the group, as printed on its notepaper (the only document it produced) were 'Holbrook Jackson (Editor of To-Day), Francis Meynell (Pelican Press), Stanley Morison (Cloister Press), B. H. Newdigate (Shakespeare Head Press), and Oliver J. Simon (Curwen Press)'. It was called 'The Fleuron'; and its head-quarters were at 10 Adam Street, Adelphi. The first meetings were held at Oliver Simon's office in St. Stephen's House, Westminster. The idea (born out of its due time) was to publish in limited editions books designed and printed by members of the partnership, who were to express their individual taste as designers. It was a practicable idea as events have proved, but the individualities of the members of the group were so pronounced that it was found impossible for them to agree on any point of choice or procedure, and before long the group dissolved into its constituent atoms. The incident was important, for out of it came the archetypal publishing houses of the new movement in printing. Oliver Simon and Stanley Morison at 'The Fleuron' (and with *The Fleuron* periodical) and Francis Meynell at the

Designed by Oliver Simon; decoration by T. Lowinsky. 7⅝″× 5¼″.

Designed and coloured by Albert Rutherston. 7¾″× 5″.

'Nonesuch' did what the original 'Fleuron' group of the Adelphi tried to do and failed.

And now, lest the pedestal grow too large for the monument, I will get down (or up) to the Double Crown Club. The Club has not itself made history. It is rather an incident, a fortunate incident, in the history I have rapidly sketched. You will have observed that nearly all the names I have given were eventually brought under the banner of the Double Crown, and that the few exceptions have been associated with the Club either as guests or readers of papers.

The trigger-act which brought the Club into being was perpetrated by Oliver Simon. He focused the scattered forces of a new movement and desired to assemble a selection of its personalities round a table with the promise of no more benefits than those which come from talking shop under agreeable circumstances. His intention was social and amiable rather than purposeful. He was, in short, at that time, an Oliver Twist rather than an Oliver Cromwell. He did not think imperially, he thought typographically. He approved also of the leading personalities of the movement and wanted more of their sort of company. He brought to his task not only his own experience of printing, but, it seemed, a fastidious taste for the right people.

His first recruit was the distinctly clubbable Hubert Foss, who added good humour and practical enthusiasm to the cause, as well as a wide knowledge of modern typography and printers. Associated with them were G. Wren Howard, Gerard Meynell, and S. C. Roberts. The first recorded incident in the Club's history reads as follows:

'The Club was originally formed at a meeting between Mr. Oliver Simon and Mr. H. J. Foss, at which it was decided provisionally to form certain rules and to elect a provisional promoting Committee. This Committee was convened for a first meeting on July 9 (1924) at the offices of the Fleuron at 101, Gt. Russell St., and there were present: Mr. Oliver Simon, Mr. G. W. Howard, Mr. Gerard

Meynell and Mr. H. J. Foss who was asked to become Hon. Sec. At the same meeting Mr. Holbrook Jackson was suggested, and later formally invited by letter, to become first President.'

The originators knew what they wanted even at that initial meeting, for they produced rules which are substantially the same as those eventually adopted. Indeed, the Club had a constitution before it had a name. No title was chosen at the next meeting (July 21st, 1924), when the Rules were submitted and the first list of proposed members was drawn up: if such a crude term can be applied to so fastidious an operation. Forty-one names were selected (excluding the six members of the committee) and of that number thirty-three became members. On July 28th, 1924, the third committee meeting was held when the subject of title was discussed and settled. The names suggested were 'Duodecimo', '32mo', 'Demy', 'Ampersand', and 'Chase'—all of which were happily abandoned for the non-committal 'Double Crown', which, in the words of the Minute recording that momentous decision, 'was proposed by Mr. G. T. Meynell, and seconded by the President, later being unanimously adopted by all members of the Committee present'. Another meeting of the Committee was held on September 23rd which fixed the Inaugural Dinner for October 31st at the Florence Restaurant. G. Wren Howard was appointed Dinner Secretary, Olive Simon Designer of the first menu-card, and the preparation of the printed matter relating to the Dinner was delegated to Gerard Meynell. The first dinner was

Centre opening of Double Crown Menu, designed by J. P. and Geoffrey Keynes. 8¼″ × 5½″.

accordingly held on that date and the discussion was devoted entirely to rules, regulations, ways, and means. Thirty-three members attended, the 'original members' present being: Hubert Foss, Gerard Meynell, S. C. Roberts, G. Wren Howard, Oliver Simon, Holbrook Jackson, C. W. Hobson, Douglas Cockerell, Bernard H. Newdigate, Graily Hewitt, Percy Smith, Frank Sidgwick, Albert Rutherston, C. H. C. Prentice, Harold Monro, T. Lowinsky, Herbert Simon, Francis Meynell, Paul Nash, Harold Curwen, Nigel de Grey, Michael Sadleir, R. W. Chapman, Humphrey Milford, Stanley Morison, Geoffrey Keynes, Harold Child, Walter Lewis, Thomas Balston, Christian Barman, A. Marrot, and Fred P. Phillips. It is worth noting as a sign of the Club's vitality that all but nine of those who took part in this first dinner are still members.

No club is immune from error, and several mistakes were made at the outset. The most memorable were idealistic. One was concerned with purpose and the other with ritual. Victims of the high-mindedness of the post-war period, we believed in improvement and new conditions. We were benevolent. We wanted to dot the *i*'s and cross the *t*'s of the new typography, and to make the printing office a place fit for typographers to live in. We had yet to learn that the only way to improve a craft is to do a job of work so well that others will be encouraged to scrounge your ideas and your methods. Imitation, not initiation, is the lubricant of progress. But I digress.

We attempted the impossible by deciding to crown

BILL OF FARE

Delicacies ☞ Mutton Broth ☞ Boiled Turbot with

Lobster Sauce ☞ Roast Turkey Mashed Chestnuts

Brussels Sprouts Roast Potatoes ☞ Ice Pudding

Sweetmeats ☞ Devils on Horseback ☞ Coffee

Designer
Holbrook Jackson

Silhouettes
The President
by Ernest August Potuczek

The Lecturer and the Designer
by Edwin Hunter, the former
after a pencil drawing by
Eric Gill

Printer
Ernest Ingham
at the Fanfare Press

The President of the Club

John Johnson

will recite the roll of

members present and their

guests, remark upon the

design of the Bill of Fare,

and ask

Francis Meynell

to address the Club on

THE NONESUCH PRESS

The Lecturer

The Designer

The President

Centre opening of Double Crown Club Menu, designed by Holbrook Jackson. 10″×8¼″.

annually the two best specimens of printing of the preceding year: one a book, and the other a specimen of
biblia a-biblia. More awards might have been decided
upon, but the Club had only two Crowns at its disposal.
The Coronation dinner nearly ended in a row before it
was realized, as the ancients realized so long ago, that
there can be no unanimity of opinion on matters of taste:

Oh, East is East and West is West,
And never the twain shall meet,
Till Earth and Sky stand presently at God's great Judgement
    Seat;
But there is neither East nor West, Border nor Breed nor
    Birth,
When two strong men stand face to face tho' they come from
    the ends of the earth![1]

In that debate there were not two, but thirty strong men,
and each of them fought passionately for his own opinion,
with the result that when the decisions were declared it
was found that the Crowns were unsuitably bestowed.
Then the storm broke out afresh, and the printed rules
governing the adjudication were altered in the vain hope
of establishing sound judgement on a staying basis. But
after one more attempt our one and only purposeful
effort was discreetly dropped.

The ritualistic bother arose out of the ticklish problem
of the Toast List. We were a dining club and admitted
guests. Were we public or private? If private, toasts were
not necessary; if public they might be. There is no rule.

[1] Quoted by permission of Mrs. Kipling and Messrs. Methuen & Co.,
Ltd., from *Barrack Room Ballads*.

But there is an unwritten rule which permits the Loyal Toast at semi-private tables. Here is a nice point both of etiquette and loyalty, and the problem, so far as the Club is concerned, remains unsolved. Presidents and Chairmen are free to follow their own tastes. During John Johnson's presidency the Toast of 'The King' was proposed and honoured without mishap regularly at each dinner. Earlier attempts, however, were not so successful, for when the first President at the first dinner proposed the same Toast there was some inconvenience. All present stood, some uncomfortably, and one member began to rise but diplomatically checked himself in mid-ascent, thus describing with his body something like a half-circle. This amiable proceeding soothed the secta-rians and thus relieved an embarrassing situation, for monarchists were under the impression that he stood and communists that he remained seated.

An inquiry into the incident was held at the next Com-mittee Meeting and a compromise was sanctioned. Toasts in future would be in honour of printers—but only of dead printers. So at the next dinner we drank to 'the Immortal Memory of Garamond'. But, somehow, it did not seem right. So after toying a little further with the notion it also was allowed to fade out.

It will be noted here that the Club does not permit Rules to impede practice. Our Rules are kept in their place. The spirit rather than the letter has been observed without endangering the constitution, but not without anomalies. For instance, the place and function of the

President have never been clearly defined. According to Rule IX, one of the Rules which have survived the erosion of time: 'The President shall *ex officio* become the Chairman of the first dinner in the year.' That rule has been strictly observed during two presidencies only; the rest

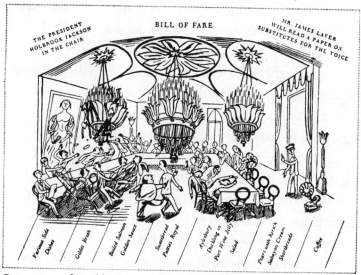

Centre page of Double Crown Club Menu, designed by Edward Bawden. $5\frac{3}{4}'' \times 8''$.

have ignored or modified it at will according to whim or convenience.

None of our Presidents has earned the description 'dictator', and no decision or ruling of the governing committee, although its membership varies every year, has been challenged by the Club. The Committee often takes the law into its own hands not because it is lawless but for the convenience of the Club. Thus without specific authority to do so it has recommended year by year successive Presidents and other officers to the Annual

General Meeting, and those recommendations have
always been accepted.

The Club has not escaped moments of unrest. Two
years ago, for instance, Oliver Simon developed what
proved to be illusions about the Club's virility. He seems

Designed and engraved by Eric Ravilious. $5\frac{1}{4}'' \times 6\frac{1}{8}''$.

temporarily to have abandoned the part of Oliver Twist
for that of Oliver Cromwell. He saw a menace in the
Double Crown. 'Take away that bauble!' he cried, in
effect. 'My personal feeling,' he wrote to President
Balston, in a letter reverently preserved in the Club's
archives, 'My personal feeling is that the Club should
gracefully expire.' The reason given was that it had 'out-
lived the impulse on which it was founded, and that new
members for one reason or another have not brought

about a marked revitalization' of its spirit. The Club, as
we know, did not expire; on the contrary the attack was
a tonic. Within a week the letter was discussed at one of
the liveliest of the Club's dinners and its proposal unanimously negatived. Nor were members slow to point the
moral and adorn the tale of this attempt at infanticide by
the Father of the Club. There are some who believe that
he did not write to slay but to save, and if that be true
he has, once again, deserved well of our select commonwealth.

It has not been the business of the Double Crown Club
to make history. The Club has been content that history
should have been made by its members, who have been
responsible for most of the events of typographical
importance in this country since 1924. And although it
has abstained from propaganda, save what comes from
personal example, it is not without admitted purpose, for
Rule II of its constitution, another rule which has never
been altered, states that the Club was formed for 'the
purpose of ex-

WILLIAM MORRIS
1834 ✿✿✿✿✿✿✿ 1934

The Forty-Third Dinner
of the Double Crown
Club, held at the Cafe
Royal, 2nd May 1934.

Mr John Johnson in the
Chair ✿✿

Morris Centenary Menu, designed in Kelmscott types by Walter Lewis. 6″ × 4⅝″.

changing ideas on good printing'. The Club obviously stands for good rather than for bad printing, though it would not confine its exchanges of ideas to one or the other. The outward and visible signs of the Club's inward and spiritual grace are the list of papers which have been read at the dinners and the names of the readers, and in the menus of those dinners, both gastronomically and typographically. The papers have covered the subject of printing in all its phases—technical, historical, aesthetic, and literary.

Forty-four papers have been read to the Club, twenty-nine of them by members or honorary members. The visiting readers have been representatives of the arts and criticism, as well as of publishing and printing. The Menu Cards form a collection unequalled in its variety and inventiveness, and valuable as representing the style of many of our leading typographical designers. These Papers and Menu Cards have all been inspired by a respect for printing and a desire to make it expressive as well as impressive; and the discussions and comments those papers and printings have provoked may, it is hoped, have contributed not a little towards the creation of a critique of typography without which we might again lapse into an era of bad printing from which our members have so recently rescued this fair land. In addition to those indications of the Club's activities, there are also a number of booklets and leaflets of various kinds presented from time to time to members by their fellow members, which further express this idea and purpose.

For the rest, dip into your memories of the printing

of ten years ago, and compare it with the printing of today....

But why seek to justify the Club? The D.C.C. is its own justification, and the only reason why it should survive is that its members enjoy its survival. It is fifty dinners old, but it is younger in spirit and vigour than at any other moment of its career. The members have every reason to thank themselves and each other. Good Printing, Good Dinners, and Good Company seem to agree with this amiable and curious cosmogony.

VI

A CROSS-SECTION OF ENGLISH PRINTING

The Curwen Press 1918–34

IT SEEMS ODD TO REFLECT THAT SCARCELY A DECADE, CER-
tainly not a decade and a half, has passed since it was
necessary to distinguish between printing and what was
called 'fine printing'. Good printing was being done by
some of the commercial presses as it had been done during
even worse typographical periods. But no one had set
about making it possible to obtain good printing for the
mere asking from the ordinary printing offices. Printing
was more or less definitely divided into two classes: the
'fine' and the 'commercial'. The one was believed to be
good; the other, to use another word then in vogue,
'practical'. The one, as a matter of fact, was the other—
in reverse.

Ten years ago 'fine printing' was still largely the stock-
in-trade of the 'private press' amateur and his many
imitators who, in Stanley Morison's words, were producing 'books that were not books from presses that were
not presses'. The inevitable result was a low average of
quality in common usage with the dubious consolation
of a succession of genuine and bastard museum pieces
for those who wanted something better and were incapable of distinguishing between what was excellent
and what was merely monumental or meretricious.

The time for a reshuffle of persons and methods was
ripe. There had been much talk and some experimenta-

tion even before 1914. Talk about printing as design was in the air, and *The Imprint* focused an argument which *The Fleuron* consummated. What happened was not so much a revolution as an evolution, which gathered impetus as it went, agglutinating this and that experience until a definite tendency could be observed. Names were associated with the change, and, for the first time in the history of printing, they were not always the names of the proprietors of the printing offices. Bernard Newdigate, Gerard Meynell, Stanley Morison, Francis Meynell, and others were thinking in terms of typographical design, examining and testing old methods as well as trying out new ones. New tastes were being formed; and a critique of printing came into being.

There were few established printers, however, who dreamt of a new era, fewer who even recognized the need for change, and still fewer who changed themselves or their plant. Of those who did Harold Curwen is inevitably spot-lighted, for he and his press are to a great extent, though not solely, responsible for that change which has made it possible for any one who desires it to procure well-designed printing, whereas before those days good printing could only be obtained by the few buyers who possessed both taste and unusual reserves of persistence.

The Curwen Press aided the growing movement by discovering and training compositors and printers who were something more than machine tenders, and allowing (even encouraging) them to do their best. It was a policy where taste was permitted to triumph over tact—the tact which succeeds by degrading.

Any one can follow a lead or a fashion once it is indicated and the pace set, but initiation is another thing. Once, for instance, movable types were invented the rest was easy. Every one probably asked why it had not been thought of before, as people always do when the inevitable happens in science or art. With the discovery of movable types printing was well on the way towards what it has since become. The limits of the craft were fixed and the principles implied. Successive changes have been largely mechanical and related to speed and cost of production rather than to taste. In each change, mechanical or aesthetic, the same laws have operated. Improvements have been no more than regenerations, corrections of lapses in taste and method. It is fortunate that regeneration is as infectious as degeneration, and that the one is always pitting itself against the other. Thus, the degeneration of printing in the nineteenth century was arrested by such men as Pickering and Morris, and thus in our own time new degenerations have been stopped and new regenerations started by the inheritors of the Pickering and Morris traditions.

Sometimes, as we have seen, fresh ideas are numerous and fertile. Epidemics of taste are familiar. But in all such periods of renaissance, even when the air itself is charged with the spirit of change, the necessary and not always welcomed disturbances can be traced back to individual sources. A renaissance is a period of theft, or mimicry, as well as a time of creative action. The only thing which is common to such periods is acceptance of the impulse whatever its origin, or in other words, the

ENGLISH

POETICAL

AUTOGRAPHS

A COLLECTION OF FACSIMILES

OF AUTOGRAPH POEMS

FROM SIR THOMAS WYAT TO

RUPERT BROOKE

SELECTED AND EDITED BY

DESMOND FLOWER AND A. N. L. MUNBY

CASSELL

AND COMPANY LIMITED

LONDON, TORONTO, MELBOURNE

AND SYDNEY

Title-page of *English Poetical Autographs.* $7\frac{1}{4}'' \times 10\frac{11}{16}''$.

generalizing of the unique. No tab has yet been tied to our contemporary renaissance of printing and I shall not attempt the task, but as time passes we can see in perspective what has happened. Names of men and presses are taking their places in something like historical order, and the achievement of the Curwen Press becomes apparent for what it is.

The press was founded in 1863 and was mainly concerned with the printing of music. In 1917 Harold Curwen, grandson of the founder, was a pupil of Edward Johnston's at the London County Council Central School of Arts and Crafts and, up to then and for a few months longer, the business was indistinguishable from other commercial presses.

The experience gained by Harold Curwen at the School of Arts and Crafts was important, for it gave a practical turn to a natural taste for design in printing. The ground was ripe for further sowing, and the new seeds were sown in a manner which was characteristic of the time and the man.

At that time Joseph Thorp had been carrying on a war of his own in favour of better lettering and printing. It was guerrilla warfare and Thorp, then as now an intellectual *franc-tireur*, went about letting off squib-like criticisms, propounding explosive propositions, and throwing admonitory bombs into the camp of the Amalekites, in the hope of startling some of the more capable of the backsliders into typographical decency. With an instinct for the right sort of man he singled out Harold Curwen, and with such success that, in 1918, Joseph Thorp became consultant of the press. The tale could be told the other way round. Curwen might have been the discoverer instead of the discovered. But knowing my Thorp as one who has been shamelessly and beneficently discovering himself to others for a number of years, I prefer to have it my own way. Anyhow, he must be credited to the Curwen account. He introduced new ideas, not least of them the introduction of Claud Lovat Fraser which led to the purchase of those charming vignettes and cover-papers which helped to give distinction to the work of the press.

In these events of fifteen years ago may be noted the two outstanding qualities which have made the Curwen Press what it is to-day. The first is the sense of good taste in printing design, and the second a readiness to make use of experts of skill and imagination and to allow them to give their talents a practical purpose. The implementation of these qualities has had that kind of success which may rightly be called unique. It has been (and still is) admirable, influential, and profitable: a most desirable consummation of any commercial enterprise, and complementary to that other unity, of materials, taste, and purpose, which has produced books satisfactory alike to amateur and expert, as well as to the general reader who is presumed, too readily, to resent and resist good printing.

The Lovat Fraser acquisition comprised a number of loose sheets covered with drawings, and a sketch-book containing some 250 drawings in all, mostly in black-and-white, suitable for vignettes and other decorations.

and later the series of small drawings made (abortively as it proved) for an edition of *A Shropshire Lad*.[1] Another purchase from the same source was a small book containing twenty-two designs for pattern papers. This collection was the basis of the Curwen range of pattern papers which has had a considerable influence on pamphlets and paper-covered books.

The Fraser period was in full flood when a further stage in the development of the press began with the appearance in 1920 out of the blue, or, more exactly, the drab of Manchester, of an unknown young man named Oliver Simon, who as Curwen typographer augmented the established typographical equipment of Harold Curwen, and in particular added book printing to the activities of the press. He soon became known and respected as a creative force in the printing arts. Without appearing to be doing much more than circulate, more or less silently, among the artistic and literary haunts of London, he brought grist to the Curwen mill in the form of new ideas, type-faces, ornaments, and above all personalities. He emulated and augmented Harold Curwen's knack of attracting outside talent, by the introduction of Albert Rutherston, whose delicately drawn and coloured decorations began to appear in 1921. The result of Rutherston's influence on illustrators is seen in the use of cross-hatching and the increasing delicacy of designing for colour line-block work.

The association of Edward Bawden with the press some

1 They were eventually published without text by the First Edition Club (1924). See pp. 211–16, *supra*.

ten years ago added further distinction to the production of work requiring decoration. His influence has been felt in practically all sections, and it includes illustrations for advertisements and booklets, as well as vignettes and other typographical ornaments, decorated cover papers and some of the wall-papers, the production of which has been a novel departure of the Press. Oliver Simon was later instrumental in bringing to the press the work of Paul Nash, Percy Smith, Enid Marx, Barnett Freedman, and other artists.

The history of this period of the press is written in the *Catalogue Raisonné of Books Printed at the Curwen Press 1920–1923*, published by the Medici Society in 1924, itself a distinguished example of the typography of the time. The object of the publication was to demonstrate the belief 'that books well designed and well printed can be produced commercially at reasonable prices'—an achievement hitherto thought possible only (or mainly) in 'limited' editions by the 'private' presses. The *Catalogue* is a document of some importance in the history of the twentieth-century renaissance of printing, for it records an incident of pronounced significance. Here is a commercial printer who is so conscious of his own integrity as a maker of books which are convenient in price and excellent in taste and construction that he does not hesitate to challenge criticism by printing an account of his book production during those four formative years, and, which is still more significant, prefacing that account with the statement that the list is not to be taken as a complete record of his work, 'but as a catalogue of books where the design and choice of materials has been freely committed to the printer'.

It was neither the intention nor the practice of the Curwen Press, however, to concentrate its effort upon book-production. One of the outstanding characteristics of the press was a recognition of the rights of all those ephemera of typography which are loosely grouped and summed up under the term 'jobbing-printing'. Harold Curwen abolished class distinctions between the printing of books and miscellaneous printing. He said, in effect, for his pronouncements have been doing rather than saying: 'Printing is one and indivisible and it must please and serve or fail.'

Under this generous influence the Cinderella of the printing arts was fitted with the missing glass slipper. Leaflets and booklets, invitation and menu cards, folders and stationery, and other press settings developed style and charm. It was as though a company of drabs had been transferred from squalor to opulence. Good jobbing-printing was not unknown at the time; but it was not generally produced or accepted, and those who wanted something better than the average production had to search for it. The Curwen Press faced the problem early and set out to satisfy, and by satisfying to increase, the then small demand for better commercial printing. Good printing is its own advertisement, and it was not long before buyers and users began to take notice.

By the beginning of the nineteen-twenties the new typographical impulsion had reached the proportions of a 'movement' whose ideas and aims demanded interpretation.

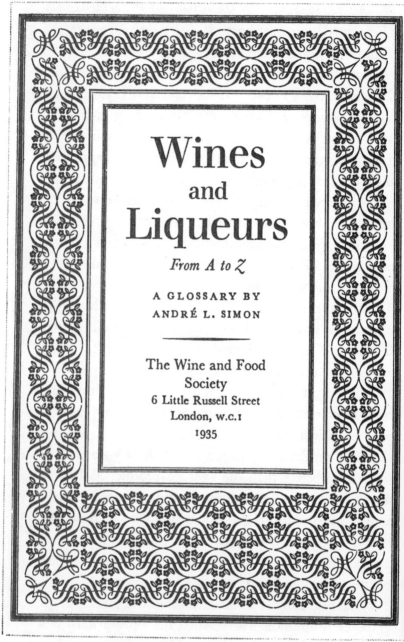

Wines
and
Liqueurs

From A to Z

A GLOSSARY BY
ANDRÉ L. SIMON

The Wine and Food
Society
6 Little Russell Street
London, w.c.1
1935

Title-page of *Wines and Liqueurs.* $7\frac{1}{2}'' \times 5''$.

THE

WESTMINSTER
BANK

THROUGH A CENTURY

By

T. E. GREGORY

ASSISTED BY ANNETTE HENDERSON

WITH A PREFACE BY

THE HON. RUPERT E. BECKETT

VOLUME I

WESTMINSTER BANK LIMITED
LONDON
1936

Title-page of *The Westminster Bank.* $7\frac{1}{2}'' \times 4\frac{3}{4}''$.

Oliver Simon took upon himself the responsibility of crystallizing the motives which were behind much scattered effort, by launching *The Fleuron* out of his own limited resources with small chance of pecuniary reward. Four numbers were produced and printed at the Curwen Press in the years 1923–5 when the adventure was transferred to Stanley Morison, who completed it in three further and final volumes which were printed at the Cambridge University Press. In these scholarly quartos the history of the period and its modes and moods are recorded in a manner which received the approval of the comparatively small body of fastidious practitioners and amateurs for whom they were issued.

The final volume of *The Fleuron* was published in 1930 and Stanley Morison was then able to note that the new activity in printing had so far developed that 'there are signs that, due allowance being made for the speculative section of the book-buying classes, the residue of readers able to distinguish good from bad typography is now sufficiently large to exert an influence upon publishers who may consequently be expected to encourage their printers in maintaining a normally high standard of craftsmanship'. *The Fleuron* mainly concerns us here as one of those periodical productions of the press which gave a new typographical distinction to magazines, later to be emphasized in the design of such periodicals as *The Woodcut*, edited by Herbert Furst (1927–30); *Life and Letters*, edited by Desmond MacCarthy (1931–3); *The Book Collector's Quarterly*, edited by A. J. A. Symons and

Desmond Flower (1930–1935); and *Wine and Food*, edited by André Simon (1934, in progress).

Principle and practice have remained united during the last decade of progress and expansion. The history of these years is for the main part written in the productions as well as in the publications of the press. Pace has been kept with the response of a public interested in printing by the introduction of new type-faces and ornaments, and the *Type Specimen Book* issued by the press is perhaps the most satisfying and complete work of the kind published in England since the War. Early advantage was taken of the Monotype revival of classical faces, the first of which, Garamond, was used in *The Fleuron*, No. I; and Baskerville, which followed shortly afterwards, was used in *The Fleuron*, No. II. In addition, the Curwen Press was the first in England to use such type-faces as Maximillian (1923), a display type, Walbaum (1925), and Koch Kursiv (1926). The range of the Curwen technique was increased when in 1927 Harold Curwen introduced into England the general use of the Stencil Process, previously used in France and elsewhere. The method of reproduction was developed at first from the study of *Traité d'Enluminure d'Art au Pochoir*, by Jean Sandé, and perfected by experience from job to job, with occasional help from the artist who had illustrated the book. Stencilling is now largely executed by girls taken almost haphazard from the bindery. Many of them took quickly to the most varied work of the process and have since developed great aptitude for it.

From time to time the work of the press has been

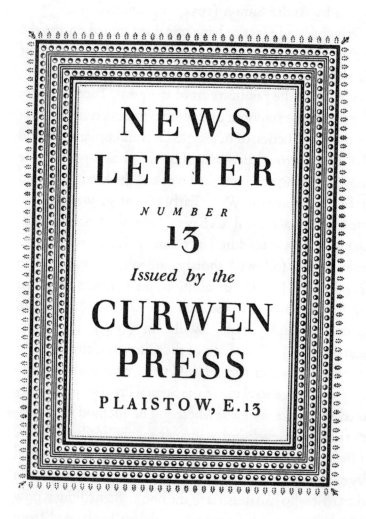

NEWS
LETTER

NUMBER
13

Issued by the

CURWEN
PRESS

PLAISTOW, E.13

Cover of Curwen Press *News Letter*. Printed in black and red on grey paper. 10¼″×7½″.

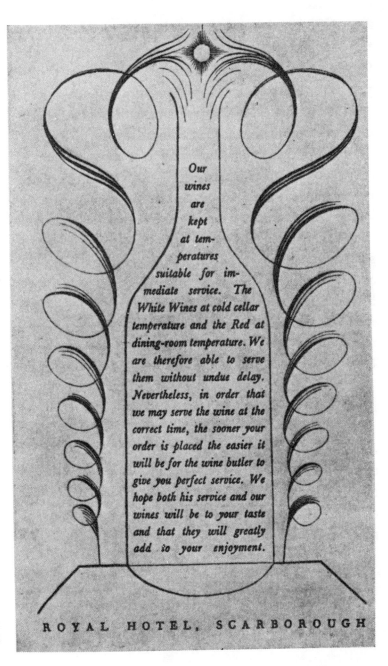

Our
wines
are
kept
at tem-
peratures
suitable for im-
mediate service. The
White Wines at cold cellar
temperature and the Red at
dining-room temperature. We
are therefore able to serve
them without undue delay.
Nevertheless, in order that
we may serve the wine at the
correct time, the sooner your
order is placed the easier it
will be for the wine butler to
give you perfect service. We
hope both his service and our
wines will be to your taste
and that they will greatly
add to your enjoyment.

ROYAL HOTEL, SCARBOROUGH

Page of Wine List, printed in red and black. $7\frac{1}{2}'' \times 4\frac{1}{2}''$.

K k

recorded in catalogues and type books, and in 1932 the Curwen Press *News Letter* was first issued. This occasional publication forms, in its typography alone, apart from any information given in the text, a graphic report of inventive progress. Each number has a different design and colouring, and in addition to examples of current types, ornaments, and lay-outs, contains articles of general and specialized interest to users of printing.

The press has never been exclusive in aim or achievement. The ideal has been to produce printing with the sort of distinction which comes with good taste in design and materials for all purposes. The scope of that work has been wide enough to include several examples of the *édition de luxe* which can only appeal to the resources of the opulent connoisseur. Such Curwen Press books as *Urne Buriall*, *The Haggadah*, *Horati Carminum*, and *The Apocrypha* were distinguished during the recent boom in limited editions.

But whether it was a menu or a folder, a leaflet or book, the standard has been the best practised by the press. To carry out such an ideal requires determination and courage as well as taste and ingenuity. These qualities are characteristic of all Curwen Press work and obvious to those who know good from mediocre printing.

1935

VII

A SANCTUARY OF PRINTING

IT IS KNOWN TO SOME OF THOSE WHO ARE CONVERSANT
with the trends of printing and the habits of printers that
Dr. John Johnson, Printer to the University of Oxford,
has for some years devoted the spare time of a full life to
the business of forming a collection of the ephemera of
printing; and, further, that his efforts have produced
results which promise to be of lasting benefit not only
to members and dependants of the craft of printing but,
in some considerable measure, to historians, sociologists,
psychologists, and indeed to all those who have to con-
duct research into events, fashions, customs, or any of the
social and intellectual movements which have found
expression in, or received aid or impetus from, printed
documents other than books.

Everybody in these days is conscious of the pervasion
of print but few who have not focused their minds upon
the subject can have any idea of its extent and variety.
Despite bulging waste-paper-baskets and littered public
places, we are in the habit of thinking of books or periodicals when we think of print; but vast as those two classes
are, the productions of the jobbing printer are greater,
more varied, and possibly more influential. It is said that
the popular newspapers have little political influence,
and that the patrician newspapers preach to the conver-
ted, but there can be little doubt that leaflet, folder, and
poster are insinuating their admonitions, whether we like
it or not, into the texture of our lives. Nations are welded

and classes levelled by propaganda and advertisement. But the ephemera of printing are not all engaged in the clamour of popular persuasion. Much jobbing printing is restrained, disinterested, and necessary, for our complex modern lives are largely conditioned by productions of this hitherto neglected class of printing.

There would be little to remark if such a collection were no more than a miscellany of typographical curiosities. But the Sanctuary of Printing, as it is called by its founder, is not merely a refuge for fallen scraps of paper or unwanted printed documents. Such a refuge might be nothing but a Gargantuan waste-paper-basket. The Sanctuary in its own way is a reference library, and it should serve much the same purpose as a library of books. Books are less easily destroyed but the contents of the majority are as ephemeral as the advertisements and announcements which form so large a part of the collection. The one differs from the other in technique, not in function. In the last resort all printed matter is advertisement and most of it commercial. But important as such advertisements are as reflections of the mind and manners of an era, as well as of the mind and feelings of individual authors, they are not the only reflections. Dr. Johnson's store of ephemera may prove to be as reliable a guide to historians as the congeries of books in the Bodleian or the British Museum. The historian of the future may yet learn more of our period from book-jackets and blurbs than from the novels whose flamboyancies are designed to sell, just as the literary archaeologist has recovered treasures of song from the ephemeral broadsides of the itinerant balladmonger.

Dr. Johnson has proved himself to be a disinterested and adventurous collector, and no accumulator of quaintnesses or rarities for their own sake. He brushes up the fallen leaves for the benefit of research. He finds sermons in folders and books in bus-tickets. Probably some desire to augment his own knowledge inspired his earliest enthusiasm for typographical oddments, but such an aim, if it ever existed, has been merged into a larger purpose. He now takes the long view and sees his specimens as members of a cosmogony of printing wherein savants may reconstruct forgotten eras from scraps of paper, as geologists have recreated the Dinotherium and the Mastodon from fragments of bone preserved in museums of natural history.

It is natural, and, indeed, inevitable, that this collection should have been formed by Dr. John Johnson, who was interested in social history and an archaeologist before he became a printer, and learnt to respect what he is not afraid to call rubbish long ago whilst digging for scraps of Greek manuscripts in the dust-heaps of ancient Egypt. At that time it was not so generally recognized as it is to-day that what was buried as rubbish may be exhumed as treasure. Some of the most valuable records of our progenitors have been rescued from the middens of prehistoric man. Rubbish is, after all, a relative term; it may be anything for which there is no immediate use; anything, in fact, may be rubbish at some time or in some place. The Victoria and Albert Museum from one point of view is largely filled with old junk. But the point at which printed matter becomes junk requires further definition. Books are surrounded by enemies. The majority of people will not allow their houses to be encumbered with them. There are even differences of bookish affection among scholars and collectors. What is one man's literature is another man's litter.

The Bodleian used to clear out its first editions as so much rubbish when new ones appeared. It thus found itself for a long period without a First Folio Shakespeare. And not much more than a hundred years ago that dependable institution refused shelfroom to Cobbett's *Weekly Register*, the *Memoirs of Oliver Cromwell*, Scott's *Antiquary*, Byron's *Siege of Corinth*, Shelley's *Alastor*, Wordsworth's *Thanksgiving Ode*, and the *Army List*! It is not surprising to learn that in view of such lapses Falconer Madan doubted 'the power of contemporaries to determine the residual value of a book'. What is more useless than the popular novel that has passed its boom! Yet, Madan assures us, not a week passed during the compilation of the *Oxford English Dictionary* without recourse to the sixty or seventy thousand Victorian novels in the British Museum and the Bodleian. First editions are no longer throw-outs, but with few exceptions every one has thrown into the waste-paper-basket the hand-bills and programmes and menu cards and folders of commercial or jobbing printing from William Caxton to Harold Curwen, regardless of the fact that they may thus have risked destroying the evidences of philology and other sciences.

The idea of the Sanctuary was born in the University Press. During the reorganization of that famous printing 'office', which Dr. Johnson undertook in 1925, he realized more and more the vitality of the tradition which had governed the press for centuries, and his respect for those historic evidences grew as he worked. He preserved what was old and memorable together with what was old and useful. But as his work proceeded he was surprised to learn that in the equipment there was an absence of anything approaching a complete collection of Oxford printing. Oxford books existed in public and collegiate libraries and on private shelves, but few were preserved in the institution where they were born. And it is not surprising that something more than regret was felt when it became known that Falconer Madan's collection of Oxford printing had been sold to Yale University. The emigration to America of that invaluable assembly was a shock for Dr. Johnson from which he recovered by resolving to make good the loss. During the search he came across specimens of all kinds of Oxford printing, and they became the nucleus from which the collections in the Sanctuary at Oxford have grown.

But here the relationship with the Press ends. The Sanctuary is an independent entity, financed heroically by its founder and a few friends, and its object is to illustrate not printing but the social history of which printing is an incident. And just as it was by the accident of Dr. Johnson's experience as an excavator in the cemeteries and rubbish mounds of ancient Egypt that he came to learn that, in his own words, 'the ephemera of to-day become the evidential data of to-morrow', so certain fortunate circumstances encouraged him whilst laying the foundations of the Sanctuary of Printing. Notable among them was the acquisition of the residuum of the collections of typographical flotsam and jetsam accumulated by three Oxford men. These predecessors were the bibliographers Robert Proctor and W. D. Macray (who wrote *The Annals of the Bodleian*), and E. W. B. Nicholson, one of Bodley's librarians.

Each of these men had a squirrel-like instinct for hoarding. Their passion was often for what is usually looked upon as waste-paper. Proctor, for instance, kept every railway- or bus-ticket he could lay hands on, and old receipts and printed paper bags had a peculiar attraction for him. Macray had a predilection for the ephemera of publishing and other forms of book distribution, such as prospectuses, library announcements, and the like. Nicholson's taste was more heterogeneous; he saw specimens in all kinds of printed matter, including his own dog licence, and probably got nearer to the idea since developed by Dr. Johnson. Unfortunately these accumulations were in an advanced state of dissolution before they reached the Sanctuary, but they were acceptable none the less, and have been profitably merged into the general scheme.

His diligence and watchfulness have again and again been rewarded by collector's luck and by coincidence. The disposal of estates often brings into the light of day a cache of waste-paper which he is thanked for removing, or a gift may come out of the blue. An interesting example illustrates the sudden augmentation of the Cigarette-Card section. Dr. Johnson was lamenting the poverty of specimens covering the early nineteen-hundreds, which were the cradle days of the craze, and he reflected dismally that almost all of them must have perished, when within a few days came a gift of 200 of the once-famous *Ogden's Guinea Gold* cards issued during the South African War. But welcome as such gifts are, no great collection was ever built on luck or generosity. Your own efforts and methods are the prime determinants. And perhaps method should come first. It is necessary, among other things, to know what you have got before you can get what you want. Fortunately Dr. Johnson brought to the adventure his own experience as an organizer. He has not only what he has called 'a miscellaneous mind'. He is equipped with a methodical mind as well. So for the first time in the curious history of the passion for accumulating scraps of printed paper the principle of classification had a chance of being applied.

The old collectors lacked the larger vision. They certainly felt that there was some value in typographical smallwares, but none of them realized that a rubbish-heap is still a rubbish-heap until it has been sorted out or classified by a lumber merchant or a scientist. Dr. Johnson is bringing order out of chaos by scientific classification.

The specimens are preserved in a room in the Oxford Press building, and arranged according to class in series of folders kept in boxes and drawers. The classes cover most of the main areas of typographic activity, beginning with bibliography and printing, which remain the most important sections, exhibiting as they do the history of printing in all its phases, with special attention to the development of books. In this section alone there is a range of drawers containing specimen *Parts* comprising more than 200 years of periodical book publication. In addition there are classes, most of them complete, containing typical examples of printed documents relating to—Dictionaries and Encyclopaedias, Authors' Societies, Publishers, Booksellers, Binders and Binding, Book Jackets, Paper Making, Title-Pages, Printers' Plant, Printers' Marks, Stationery, General Typography, Libraries, Publicity, and Copyright, together with a long series of specimens illustrating the Fourdrinier papers.

A large class specializes in Prospectuses, Type-Specimen Books, Specimen Pages, and other documents relating specifically to printing presses commercial and private, ancient and modern. In the modern section alone about 150 presses and individual typographers are represented. There are also folders containing modern American, French, German, and other continental presses. The Book Prospectus class, the most complete of its kind, is housed in a dozen boxes and each specimen is mounted on a card. The greater number were printed before 1820, and will eventually be arranged in chronological sequence, preceding wherever possible the folders of the presses. There are fourteen boxes of Prospectuses of Newspapers and other Periodicals including all varieties from the earliest days of the periodical press to the present time. In addition there is a sub-section of special prospectuses arranged under Authors. This interesting feature includes a unique collection relating to Shakespeare, together with useful and growing musters of specimens referring to Samuel Johnson, Walter Scott, Thomas Frognall Dibdin, John Ruskin, Robert Bridges, Oscar Wilde, Bernard Shaw, and Gordon Craig.

One of the most important of all classes is devoted to First Numbers of periodicals, classified under no less than fifty-eight headings, and dating from the seventeenth century to the present year. It is unnecessary to enumerate the classes as they include every imaginable kind of periodical, whether news, specialist, or general, daily, weekly, or monthly.

Jobbing Printing *per se* has a section to itself. Here may be found such small fry as Tickets in astonishing variety, Invitation Cards, Note-headings, Envelopes and Wrappers, Menus and Visiting Cards. There is an impressive section devoted to Dance Programmes, another of no less than twenty boxes to Theatre Programmes, and one large case to Play Bills. The Sheet Almanack and Cartoon collections are growing up, and an important section dealing with Maps is in process of formation. Trade Cards are grouped in thirteen boxes, covering thirty-nine trades. Near by are six boxes of Bookplates, nine of Christmas Cards, and eleven of Valentines, including Tuer's own collection of Valentine Proofs in two volumes.

Book Illustration is dealt with in fifty folders containing examples cut out of periodicals and books and pasted on to sheets of hand-made paper. This collection is grouped under names of artists. It is particularly strong in the pictorial work of last century, especially the earlier periods. The wood engravers of the sixties are well represented. The aim is to bring the specimens further forward past the romantic nineties down to the futurists, cubists, and sur-realists of to-day.

The Official Section is extensive and of definite historical value. The British Post Office is represented by ten albums containing typical specimens of the innumerable documents issued in connexion with Postage, Telephone, Money Registration, and Savings Bank affairs, with an up-to-date album illustrating the development of Air Mail.

An allied service is an impressive collection of Banknotes arranged alphabetically by towns in five large leather-bound albums, and another exhibit showing the development of Cheques. Under Naval, Military, and Police there is a growing body of documents. Three boxes are devoted to the Great War, one each to the South African War, Police and Prisons, Crime, and Army General and Navy General. Advertisements are comprehensively exhibited in fifteen sections mainly classified under trades, services, and towns. Four albums are devoted to Lotteries; twenty-two to Travel and Transport from Stage Coaches to Aeroplanes; and nineteen to Amusements where you will find documentary evidence of Cosmoramas, Dioramas, and Panoramas, as well as Human Freaks, Waxworks, Fun Fairs, and Cinemas. One box contains Playing Cards and Indoor Games. And finally under Social and Economic are eleven boxes providing raw material about Women's Suffrage, Archaeology, Money, Education, Art, Music, Drama, Wireless, and the B.B.C.

The value of such a collection is obvious, but it is not confined to the interests of the general historian. Dr. Johnson is conscious of the useful purposes his Sanctuary may serve, and he believes, and those who have examined his collections agree, 'that in the future, typographers who wish to write on typographic developments of this century and last century, social historians who wish to research into the economics of trade, will alike have to turn aside to visit the material' preserved by him, 'which used to be called rubbish'.

It is already proving of increasing value to members of the printing craft. In the short period of the existence of the Sanctuary it has been the parent of six books on as many phases of printing, and will as time goes on inspire many more. It is here in fact, within folders labelled Stanley Morison, John Johnson, Oliver Simon, Francis Meynell, Eric Gill, Nonesuch, Fleuron, Shenval, and Fanfare, that the raw material exists for the history of the English renaissance of printing in our own time.[1]

Indeed the existence of the Sanctuary may do for the history of printing what Green did for the history of the English people, for it is just as shortsighted to base typographical history upon the making of books as it was to base human history upon the ambitions of kings and the progress of their wars. The much maligned John Bagford

[1] For a complete classification of the Johnsonian collection see 'Desiderata for the Sanctuary of Printing', by Vivian Ridler, *Signature* (March 1937).

had the right conception when he formed his notorious scrapbooks not only of title-pages as is too readily believed, but of a variety of typographical ephemera, for the purpose of illustrating the history of printing. The jobbing printer has made a more varied and perhaps more vital contribution to that history than the printer of books—and, in England at least, he has a more ancient lineage, for William Caxton himself was a jobbing printer before he ventured upon the production of books.

The Sanctuary of Printing at Oxford is perhaps above all things a contribution to ethnology, for however trivial the contents of its boxes and folders, those scraps of paper are authentic records of customs and superstitions, and are thus the raw material from which scientists and historians may find hints and facts which may help them to explain men's actions and thoughts. Such records could not have come into existence unless they had answered or expressed fundamental human traits. It is no exaggeration to call 'commercial art', which plays so significant a part in jobbing printing, the folk-lore of an age which tends more and more to think by proxy and to be moved by advertisement.

A large number of men and women read nothing but the ephemera of printing. Their literature is not books nor even newspapers but advertisements and other 'copy' in the form of folders, leaflets, captions, headlines, and blurbs. As a matter of fact we are all dependent for the bulk of our ideas upon print in one form or another, and ephemera in the Johnsonian sense are not always trivial. Printing is necessary to affairs of any kind, and few waking hours pass without our using some sort of printed business paper—bills, dockets, catalogues, programmes, menu cards, and the thousand and one typographical gadgets which have become so common as to be unobserved for anything save their immediate purpose. Such documents show what people, common as well as exclusive, are thinking about, and what politicians and profiteers wish them to think about.

The ephemera of printing in times past served, without undue emphasis, some immediate and often local purpose. They were more personal and circumscribed than they are to-day. But with the development of communications the tendency has been towards more universal and more and more impressive methods of persuasion. The Sanctuary contains, among other things, the records of the spread of mechanized and propagandaed civilization, together with the records in ephemeral printed matter of an older culture which may become more and more of an anachronism in an environment from which chance and idiosyncrasy are being eliminated by the management of habits and the standardization of thought. These changes are clearly reflected in the mirror provided for us by the jobbing printer, whose history has yet to be written and whose place in history has yet to be appreciated.

It is not easy to exaggerate the sociological and historical value of a collection of this kind, at a time when the minutiae of human behaviour are regarded with growing interest by those who would throw light upon life and destiny. The method of history is as mutable as humanity and its materials change with circumstances. These circumstances are no longer affected solely by will or whim but by mechanical inventions. It is only sixty years since John Richard Green, in the Preface to his *Short History of the English People*, explained that history was not entirely an affair of military and naval manœuvres, and that he had ventured to 'find a place for figures little heeded in common history—the figures of the missionary, the poet, the printer, the merchant, or the philosopher'. Dr. Johnson has provided material for the historian who may desire to find a place for the people as they are affected by the printed appeals of those who have designs upon their suffrages, their ambitions, or their purses.

1935

NOTES

NOTES

like gunpowder and the magnet. Bacon's idea was elaborated by George Hakewill (1578–1649). The extract is taken from the second edition of the *Apologie* which first appeared in 1627, the year after Bacon's death:

'Printing alone may easily contend for the prize with all the inventions of the *Ancients*. And *Polidore Virgill* having spoken of the famous Libraries erected by the Ancients, presently addes, *Fuit illud omnino magnum mortalibus munus, sed nequaquam conferendum cum hoc quod nostro tempore adepti sumus, reperto novo scribendi genere: tantum enim uno die ab uno homine literarum imprimitur, quantum vix toto anno à pluribus scribi possit.* That was indeede a great benefit to mankinde, but not to be compared with this which our age hath found out and injoyed, since a new kinde of writing was brought to light and practised, by meanes whereof, as much may be printed *by one man in one day,* as could be written by *many in a whole yeare*; or as *Sabellicus,* as much as the *readiest pen-man could well dispatch in two yeares.* And by this meanes, bookes which were before in a manner confined to the Libraries of *Monasteries,* as their only *Magazines,* were redeemed from bondage, obtained their inlargement, and freely walked abroad in the light; so as now they present themselues familiarly to the eyes and hands of all men, and he that hath but slender meanes, may notwithstanding furnish himselfe in a competent manner, there being now more good *Authours* to bee bought for *twenty shillings* then could then bee purchased for *twenty pounds.* And besides, they then spake such *languages* as it pleased the *Monkes* to put into their mouths, who many times thorow ignorance, or negligence, or wilfulness mistooke words and sentences, and sometimes thrust that into the *Text* which they found in the *Margine.* From whence arose such a confusion in most *Authours* that it much puzled the best wits how to restore them to the right sense, as *Lodovicus Vives* complaines, it befell him in the setting forth of S. *Augustines* workes *de Civitate Dei, & divinandum saepenumero fuit, & conjecturis vera restituenda Lectio*: I was often forced to guesse at the sense & none otherwise then by conjectures could the text be restored to the true reading: And *Erasmus* in his preface to the workes of the same father, *vix in alterius tam impiè quàm in hujus sacri Doctoris voluminibus lusit otiosorum temeritas,* hardly hath the rashnes of idle braines so impiously played it's part in the volumes of any other, as of this holy *Doctour*: Yet that other complaint of his in his preface before S. *Hieromes* workes, touching the many and grosse corruptions which therein hee found, farre exceedes this, *Unum illud & verè dicam & audacter, minoris arbitror Hieronymo suos constituisse libros conditos, quàm nobis restitutos*: This one thing may I truly and boldly affirme, that in mine opinion, S. *Hieromes* bookes cost him lesse paines the making, then mee the mending. *Againe*, it cannot be denied but the faireness of the letter beyond that of ordinary writing, addes no small grace to this invention. *Mira certè Ars*, sayth *Cardane, quâ mille chartarum una die conficiuntur, nec facile est judicare an in tanta facilitate ac celeritate pulchritudo, an in tanta pulchritudine celeritas & facilitas sit admirabilior*: An admirable Art sure it is, by which a thousand sheets may be dispatcht in a day; neither is it easie to judge whether in so great easinesse and quicknesse of dispatch the fairenes of the letter, or in the fairenesse of the letter the quicknesse of dispatch and easinesse thereof, be more to be wondred at. *Lastly*, it is not the least benefit of Printing, that by dispersing a number of *Copies* into particular mens hands, there is now hope that good letters shall neuer againe suffer so vniversall a decay as in former ages they haue done, by the burning and spoyling of publique *Libraries*, in which the whole treasure of learning was in a manner stored vp. Since then by this meanes; bookes are become both *fairer*, and *cheaper*, and *truer*, and *lesse subject to a totall perishing*: and since by this *Art* the *preseruer of Arts*, the Acts & writings of worthy men are made famous and commended to posterity; it were a point of haynous ingratitude to suffer the *Inventor* thereof to be buried in obliuion.' George Hakewill, Dr. of Divinitie & Arch Deacon of Surrey, *An Apologie or Declaration of the Power and Providence of God in the Gouernment of the World* (1630), 275–6.

PAGE 32. *inspired recent good printing.* The extent of Cobden-Sanderson's anticipations of recent printing theory is revealed in the following extracts from three contemporary authorities who have elaborated but not changed the basic principle so concisely defined by him:

'Typography may be defined as the craft of rightly disposing printing material in accordance with specific purpose; of so arranging the letters, distributing the space, and controlling the type as to aid to the maximum the reader's comprehension of the text.' Stanley Morison, 'First Principles of Typography', *The Fleuron* (1930), vii. 61. (Reprinted in book form 1936.)

'The reasonable producer of books starts with the principle that it is the reading, not the reading matter, which determines the size of book and style of type; the other considerations come in only as modifying influences. In planning a book the first questions are: who is going to read this, and under what circumstances?' Eric Gill, *An Essay on Typography* (1931), Second Edition (1936), 106.

'Competence in printing is something other than the conscious search for fine printing; so-called fine printing almost always ending in isolation, or at best in experimentation. In books which are meant for the reader experiment must always be subordinate to the subject of the book and the ability of the reader; it must never disconcert or obtrude itself into the mind of the reader.' John Johnson, *The Printer, his Customers, and his Men* (1933), 50.

PAGE 33. *the modern typographer.* 'A new force in the shape of the Typographer has arrived. He is, for good or evil, that typical twentieth-century product—the specialist. He concerns himself exclusively with the designing of printing, the assembling of appropriate types, the choice of paper, ink, ornament, and binding, &c., for the book in hand. He is sometimes, but too rarely, to be found in the person of the master printer himself; more usually he is an outsider co-opted on to the staff. In the latter case he is free from administrative and financial cares, and it is claimed that his strength and usefulness and particular scope lie in this detachment, which enables him to innovate and change. In England the Typographer is sometimes to be found directing from a Publishers' office, a fact which does not compliment the professionals. We may at any rate be thankful that the Typographer, wherever he is, is definitely in the "trade", and not a cultivated amateur of means, living and working divorced from the Press by distance and outlook.

'The position of the Typographer has its dangers. It leads somewhat easily to a facile eclecticism, very easy to acquire, and readily acclaimed by a large section of the book-loving public, which in its innocence is ever ready to confound the antique and curious with the beautiful. But one factor, perhaps more than any other, has made the Typographer necessary in England if English printing is to have a future. I refer to the Trades Unions, which have, it would appear, reached their finest point of organization (another form of specialization), achieved for the ever necessary purpose of economic defence and offence. Each process of printing has its well-drilled, massed, but exclusive and water-tight compartment of workers, helpless and unorganized to achieve printing results of any aesthetic value without the Typographer to watch, guide, and lead them. The twentieth century has completed the transition from the hand to the machine.' Oliver Simon, *Printing of To-Day* (1928), 10–11.

PAGE 47. *the awakening of typographical taste*. The criticism of printing began before the nineties as the following extract from a lecture delivered in 1882 proves:

'Who spoils our new English books? It is manifest that there are no less than ten parties directly interested in this question, and that one, several, or all of them may justly be accused if not convicted as participants in the decadence of book-making in England.
'They are,

1. The Author,
2. The Publisher,
3. The Printer,
4. The Reader,
5. The Compositor,
6. The Pressman or Machinist,
7. The Paper-maker,
8. The Ink-maker,
9. The Book-binder, and
10. The last not least, the Consumer, often ignorant and careless of the beauty and proportions of his books—a great sinner!

'Now of all these ten sinners by omission or commission it is no business of ours to point out who is the greatest or the least. Any one of them can spoil a good book in spite of the combined efforts and merits of the other nine. But when two or three unite in their ignorance and mechanical blindness, nothing but accident can save the book.
'There is, however, no question of honesty or dishonesty in the

matter. All and every one of the ten co-labourers are willingly credited with good intentions, but there is somehow at the present day a painful lack of harmony apparent in the results, the bungling work of one of them, or the clumsy manipulation of another, often defeating the combined excellence of all the rest. Indeed, no book can be perfect in its manufacture unless every stage of it be guarded by sanctified common sense.

'Our new books at their present prices are not what they should be. Is it not time therefore for Librarians, whose business is dissemination, and whose occupation is "books", to set their Association thinking of the subject? The cure is not to be effected in a giffin. The matter must be looked into and fought out until there be established "A School of Typography" in England, in which every disciple of these ten tribes shall study a recognized grammar of book-manufacture, including printing, as standard as Lindley Murray's, Noah Webster's, or the British Museum ninety-one Rules for Cataloguing. Let every one of the ten learn his rules and play well his part, and then the art of bookmaking will drift back into the practice of those same laws of proportion, taste, and workmanship so well settled and displayed in old manuscripts and old books, large and small, long before and long subsequent to the birth of typography.' *Who Spoils Our New English Books*, Asked and Answered by Henry Stevens of Vermont (1884). Originally read before the Library Association, Cambridge, October 1882.

PAGE 52. *Robert Burton had typographical taste.* 'The Anatomy of Melancholy is one of those books which possess something like human character and behaviour, the kind of book which seems to have grown. Few books are more definitely or more curiously imbued with their authorship. The *Anatomy* is Burton, and Burton the *Anatomy*. To read it is to read him: to read him is to talk with him, to know him as we know the great persons of fiction, or those few writers who have so projected themselves into their works as to have achieved for their own personalities what the great novelists and dramatists have achieved for the characters of their stories and plays. Burton, like Montaigne, Pepys, and Lamb, has made a fiction of himself, stranger and more interesting than fact.

'It was born in 1621, when Burton was forty-five: a small quarto, of nearly nine hundred pages, exceedingly plump for its size. During the following seventeen years it continued to grow and improve through four editions, 1624, 1628, 1632, and 1638, each in small folio, but, after the author's death in 1639–40, decline began. Inferior printing and paper set in with the edition of 1651, the first reprint after Burton's death and the last to contain his corrections. In 1660 another edition appears, still more degenerate in character, and the seventeenth-century editions end with the lanky folio of 1676, from which all charm and character have gone. There were no further editions for a hundred and twenty-four years. No book of the century exhibits more clearly the personal influence of author upon printer. The hand of Burton is revealed in all the editions up to 1638. There are innumerable changes, often small and even whimsical, sometimes considerable, which bear evidence of a taste and fancy other than what at that time spontaneously issued even from the Oxford printing office. The author, true bookman as he was, must have had many an exciting wrangle with his publisher, Henry Cripps, and Leonard Lichfield, "Printer to the famous University", coming out, as I gather, victoriously, for he has contrived also to leave his own mark upon the typography of the book into which he had put so much of himself.' Holbrook Jackson, Introduction to *The Anatomy of Melancholy* by Robert Burton, Everyman's Library (1932), pp. xiii–xiv.

PAGE 85. *first to discover whether it is legible or not.* One of Ruskin's outstanding characteristics is carefulness. He was a master of detail and may be presumed to have taken as much care of the printing of his words as he did of the reproduction of his drawings. The two interests are combined in these extracts from the Prefaces to *The Stones of Venice* and *The Two Paths*, and they also reveal his concern for the convenience of his readers:

'It was of course inexpedient to reduce drawings of crowded details to the size of an octavo volume—I do not say impossible, but inexpedient; requiring infinite pains on the part of the engraver, with no result except further pains to the beholder. And as, on the other hand, folio books are not easy reading, I determined to separate the text and the unreducible plates. I have given, with the principal text, all the illustrations absolutely necessary to the understanding of it, and, in the detached work, such additional text as had special reference to the larger illustrations.

'A considerable number of these larger plates were at first intended to be executed in tinted lithography; but, finding the result unsatisfactory, I have determined to prepare the principal subjects for mezzotinting—a change of method requiring two new drawings to be made of every subject: one a carefully penned outline for the etcher, and then a finished drawing upon the etching. This work does not proceed fast, while I am also occupied with the completion of the text; but the numbers of it will appear as fast as I can prepare them.

'For the illustrations of the body of the work itself, I have used any kind of engraving which seemed suited to the subjects—line and mezzotint, on steel, with mixed lithographs and woodcuts, at considerable loss of uniformity in the appearance of the volume, but, I hope, with advantage, in rendering the character of the architecture it describes. And both in the plates and the text I have aimed chiefly at clear intelligibility: that any one, however little versed in the subject, might be able to take up the book, and understand what it meant forthwith. I have utterly failed of my purpose, if I have not made all the essential parts of the essay intelligible to the least learned, and easy to the most desultory readers, who are likely to take interest in the matter at all.' John Ruskin, *The Stones of Venice* (1851), Preface.

'Here is another of my books republished at the request of my earnest and kind friend, Mr. Henry Willett; a statement especially due to him, because, in glancing over the sheets as reissued, I find them full of useful things which I did not know I had said, and should probably have wasted much time in saying again; and I am therefore heartily glad that these four lectures are again made generally readable.

'I have no time nor sight now, however, for the revision of old plates: what my eyes can do, must be fresh work: and besides, I own to a very enjoyable pride in making the first editions of my books valuable to their possessors, who found out, before other people, that these writings and drawings really *were* good for something. I have retained therefore in this edition only the woodcuts necessary for the explanation of the text: and the two lovely engravings by Messrs. Cuff and Armytage will, I hope, render the old volume more or less classical among collectors. They were merely its ornaments, and the few references to them are withdrawn from the present edition without the slightest harm to its usefulness.

'In other respects, I doubt not my publisher's care has made it, what it professes to be, an absolute reprint of the former text.' John Ruskin, *The Two Paths* (1878), Preface.

PAGE 86. *the real good of all work* . . . This sociological attitude towards aesthetics is applied to books in the following passage from the Preface to the 1871 edition of *Sesame and Lilies*:

'The first Lecture says, or tries to say, that, life being very short, and the quiet hours of it few, we ought to waste none of them in reading valueless books; and that valuable books should, in a civilized country, be within the reach of every one, printed in excellent form, for a just price; but not in any vile, vulgar, or, by reason of smallness of type, physically injurious form, at a vile price. For we none of us need many books, and those which we need ought to be clearly printed, on the best paper, and strongly bound. And though we are, indeed, now a wretched and poverty-struck nation, and hardly able to keep soul and body together, still, as no person in decent circumstances would put on his table confessedly bad wine, or bad meat, without being ashamed, so he need not have on his shelves ill-printed or loosely and wretchedly-stitched books; for, though few can be rich, yet every man who honestly exerts himself may, I think, still provide, for himself and his family, good shoes, good gloves, strong harness for his cart or carriage horses, and stout leather binding for his books. And I would urge upon every young man, as the beginning of his due and wise provision for his household, to obtain as soon as he can, by the severest economy, a restricted, serviceable, and steadily—however slowly—increasing, series of books for use through life; making his little library, of all the furniture in his room, the most studied and decorative piece; every volume having its assigned place, like a little statue in its niche, and one of the earliest and strictest lessons to the children of the house being how to turn the pages of their own literary possessions lightly and deliberately, with no chance of tearing or dogs' ears.' *Sesame and Lilies*, by John Ruskin (1871), Preface.

PAGE 92. *Whistler must have brooded over his pages.* 'Whistler was constantly at the Ballantyne Press, where the book was printed. He chose the type, he spaced the text, he placed the Butterflies, each of which he designed to convey a meaning. They danced, laughed, mocked, stung, defied, triumphed, drooped wings over the farthing damages, spread them to fly across the Channel, and expressed every word and every thought. He designed the title-page; a design contrary to established rules, but with the charm, the balance, the harmony, the touch of personality he gave to everything, and since copied and prostituted by foolish imitators who had no conception of its purpose. Mr. MacCall, of the Ballantyne Press, has told us of his interest and has a proof of it in a collection of Butterflies and proof sheets covered with Whistler's corrections. Here, too, as everywhere by those he worked with, he is remembered with affection, and the printers were delighted to profit by his suggestions.' E. R. and J. Pennell, *The Life of James McNeill Whistler*, revised edition (1911), 291.

PAGE 104. *designed types to express his own theories of phonetics.* One of the earliest of his experiments was made with English quantitative hexameters in *Now in Wintry Delights*, printed at the Daniel Press (1903), and the poet's interest in this sort of pioneer work continued for the rest of his life, his latest conclusions appearing in the *Testament of Beauty*. John Johnson refers to the work on phonetics in his note on 'Robert Bridges and the Oxford University Press' (1930):

'His interest in phonetics, shown in *Now in Wintry Delights*, led him in 1902 to persuade his friend Edward Johnston to help in designing the extra vowels required for a phonetic alphabet. Later, with his wife, and Mr. Horace Hart, he based a new phonetic alphabet on the Elstob Anglo-Saxon eighteenth-century lettering in types of the Press. The varied letters of this alphabet seemed to him to have something of the freedom of manuscript, and he saw that new letters could be devised which would consort happily with the existing company.

'In the designing of *Ibant Obscuri* he abandoned this fount (the book had in any case become too long for it), and went back to his first love of Fell type, taking especial pleasure in the picturesque ligatures of the Greek.

'But he was to make another, and more successful, attempt at a phonetic alphabet. When the University Press approached him in 1926 to allow them to publish an edition of his Prose Works, he replied that he would consent if they would let him spell as he liked. By this time he was in touch with Mr. Stanley Morison and grafted the many phonetic symbols on to the Monotype Blado Italic. This adapted type is now known as the Chilswell fount, after his home, and has been used in four numbers of his Collected Essays.

'Perhaps the strongest reason for his interest in phonetics was his concern at the degradation of our speech and his fear that degraded forms might be stereotyped by a misuse of phonetic. This was the theme of a paper "On the Present State of English Pronunciation" printed in 1910 in *Essays and Studies*, subsequently reprinted in 1913 with notes and explanations as *A Tract on the Present State of English Pronunciation*.'

PAGE 110. *interest in actual processes of printing.* Since the chapter on George Moore was written further information of his interest in typography has been published, particularly in Joseph Hone's *Life* (1936). Moore's growing interest in all the details of the architecture of books is further exemplified, and more especially his flirtation with illustrators. As far back as 1886 he had toyed with the idea of a frontispiece by his friend J. E. Blanche for *A Drama in Muslin*, and that artist actually designed the cover for the first edition of the *Confessions of a Young Man*. His interest in covers went little farther than the grey boards with vellum spines of the limited edition, and the marbled paper imitation half-bound treatment of *The Brook Kerith* (1916), later adopted for the Uniform Edition. The desire for illustrated or decorated editions of his works developed as he grew older, and there was an abortive attempt to illustrate *The Lovers of Orelay* first by Tonks and afterwards, on Tonks's recommendation, by Rex Whistler, then a little-known student at the Slade. Tonks believed Rex Whistler would 'make Moore's book, just as Tenniel made *Alice in Wonderland*'. There appears to have been a difference of opinion between author and artist on the method of interpreting the story, Rex Whistler's drawings seeming 'to reveal something in the book hidden to Moore'. The illustrations for *The Brook Kerith* with engravings by Stephen Gooden had a happier termination. Moore liked to pride himself on having discovered Gooden, and was displeased when he learned that Tonks had known the engraver at the Slade.

'At first', says Mr. Hone, 'all went well between Mr. Moore and Gooden, and an engraving as a frontispiece for *Ulick and Soracha* was accepted after some criticism. But in the matter of *The Brook Kerith* Gooden showed a proper desire that his own interests should be respected, and made the business-like arrangement that he should produce so many illustrations. Moore then, as one could have foretold, began to criticize the designs, and said disagreeable things about them. Gooden was not in the least disconcerted, and continued with the work, and gradually Tonks noticed that as Moore received the proofs he became more and more inclined to praise them, until finally he became Gooden's most devoted admirer.' *Life of George Moore*, 406.

It was not long before he described one of Gooden's engravings of a cock for *Peronnik the Fool* as the finest ever done in England, and in *A Communication to my Friends* he hoped that one day 'when I am among the gone' his publisher would ask Gooden to do five or six pictures for his *Daphnis and Chloe*, and he said, 'should such a thing happen I doubt not that God will open my ears to hear the crowing of the cock'.

PAGE 119. *almost convict him of profiteering.* 'George Moore has seldom endured injuries in silence, and I have already alluded to his resentment—perfectly just and perfectly vain—of the attitude of the libraries towards certain of his books. In those books he challenged the world, and the world replied in its old dull-eared way that makes recrimination useless. But there is something finer than resentment in his regard for his calling: there is pride, and a jealousy for the honour of English letters; and although it does not persuade him into muting his tongue to shy whispers and becoming as other men (and therefore less himself), it secures him against worse than casual lapses. His pride extends to the outward form of a book, demanding the same conscience in the type-founding, type-setting, and paper-making as he has himself come to observe in the diligent art of an author. *The Brook Kerith* showed the first and admirable sign of his rare concern, but *A Story-Teller's Holiday* is a better as well as a more costly example. The suggestion having been made that in issuing expensive and fine books he is actuated only by a spirit of gain, he answers: A strange charge to bring against a man who has worked for thirty years, week in, week out, at a craft in which he is considered a mastercraftsman by common consent without ever making two thousand a year, very rarely one thousand, more often merely a few hundreds! He adds, " Let none read in this statement a complaint of injustice done to me. My recompense is the full enjoyment of my craft, and in circumstances so favourable that it is often a wonder to me that I did not do better than I have done. To escape from useless regret I fall to thinking of the difficulties that beset every man who goes forth with an ideal in his mind." ' John Freeman, *A Portrait of George Moore in a Study of his Work* (1922), 201.

PAGE 122. *generally ignorant substitutes for colons.* The article has appeared in booklet form, without permission, and Bernard Shaw has disclaimed responsibility for the reprint, which has now been withdrawn. A review of the booklet appeared in *The Observer* in 1921, and it drew from Bernard Shaw the following disclaimer in a letter to the editor of that journal:

'Sir,—As the review in your issue of the 21st under the above title has led many persons to believe that I have written a book entitled *On Modern Composition*, will you allow me to say that I have done nothing of the sort. What has happened is that somebody has dug up an old note of mine on printing which appeared years ago in a trade paper, and has reprinted it in pamphlet form as an advertisement. As it seems that the parties to this audacious piracy have acted in that invincible ignorance of the laws of literary propriety which is a national characteristic in this country, I refrain from giving their names, or making them walk their own plank; but the issue of the pseudo-treatise on composition has been stopped; and I appeal to the public to stop telephoning me about it, and placing orders with their booksellers that can never be executed. Faithfully, G. Bernard Shaw, 10, Adelphi Terrace, London, W.C. June 16, 1921.'

PAGE 161. The two publications of the Romney Street Press are:

1. *Ten Poems by Alice Meynell 1913–1915.* Westminster, The Romney Street Press, 1915. 16 pp. Small 4to. It was sold by John Libble, the Serendipity Shop, 46 Museum Street, W.C. 'John Libble' was the late Everard Meynell, the printer's brother and the biographer of Francis Thompson. The prospectus describes the book in the following words: 'Of these Poems fifty copies have been printed in the Fell type on hand-made paper by Francis Meynell. Each copy has ten written initials by Edward Johnston.

The whole edition save five copies is for sale; bound in limp vellum, price £1 11s. 6d. each, or wrappered in Italian coloured paper, price £1 5s. 0d. each. The day of publication will be December 21st, and orders should be sent to Mr. Libble without delay; for copies will only be bound as they are ordered, and the binding will take at least one week.' In addition to the ten initials by Edward John-ston there is a paragraph mark on p. 8, and under the colophon the words 'Rubricated by Edward Johnston December 1915'. It is perhaps due to the time of publication (the second year of the Great War) rather than to any lack of appreciation on the part of collec-tors or readers that, as Francis Meynell tells us in *The Nonesuch Century*, the fifty copies of this beautiful pamphlet were only 'disposed of . . . with a good deal of difficulty'. I still rejoice that I was one of the original purchasers and that I got my copy 'wrap-pered in Italian coloured paper' from Mr. Libble himself.

2. *Meditations from the Note Book of Mary Carey 1649–1657.* Printed and sold by Francis Meynell, 67 Romney Street, West-minster, 1918. 54 pp. 32mo. wrappered in coloured paper. One hundred copies were printed in Fell Type, 'In April of the year 1918 being the fifth year of the war'. The Printer writes the Preface, and the Dedication reminds us again of the War: 'If the printer has any right of dedication, then: To Lilias and to Robert in prison.'

PAGE 165. *architects of books rather than builders.* The amount of care devoted to the production of the Nonesuch books is obvious, but the following two notes selected from among many in the *Lists* of the Press are further evidence of the affectionate deliberation which attended the making of the books:

Pope's Homer: 'The book . . . has about 100 pages of thin but crisp and sympathetic paper, made to a very light grey colour; is set in type made most delicately flexible in its inter-linear spacing by the expedient of setting it on no less than four different "point" systems, out of which it has proved possible to humour the necessi-ties of each and every one of the twenty-four books individually; and, finally, has head pieces made up of small Homeric figurines, ornaments, architectural motives, designed as types (and composed as types into dramatic episodes) especially for this book by Professor Rudolf Koch—the finest type designer of our day.' *Prospectus and Retrospectus of the Nonesuch Press* (1930).

Dryden's Complete Dramatic Works: 'The Nonesuch edition, published to commemorate the tercentenary of Dryden's birth, will be in style a modification of its Congreve, Wycherley, Otway, Farquhar, et caetera. This is to say, the volume will be the same height on the shelf (ten and a quarter inches) but the page will be one inch narrower, saving it from that wearisome expanse of blank margins which would have been due to the short verse line of the majority of Dryden's dramas. The quarto page was designed for Restoration comedy: the page of the Dryden is redesigned to suit the shorter line of Heroic Drama.' *Prospectus of the Nonesuch Press* (1931).

INDEX